EDITOR: LEE JOHNSON

## NEW VANGUARD

# FLAMMPANZER
## GERMAN FLAMETHROWERS
## 1941-1945

*Text by*
TOM JENTZ *and* HILARY DOYLE
*Colour plates by*
PETER SARSON

First published in Great Britain in 1995 by
Osprey, an imprint of Reed Consumer Books Ltd.
Michelin House, 81 Fulham Road,
London SW3 6RB
Auckland and Melbourne

ISBN 1 85532 547 0

Page design: the Black Spot
Filmset in Great Britain
Printed through World Print Ltd., Hong Kong

*For a catalogue of all books published by
Osprey Military please write to:*

The Marketing Manager, Consumer Catalogue
Department, Osprey Publishing Ltd, Michelin House, 81
Fulham Road, London SW3 6RB

## Artist's Note

Readers may care to note the original paintings from which
the colour plates in this book were prepared are available
for private sale. All reproduction copyright whatsoever is
retained by the publisher. All enquiries should be
addressed to:

Peter Sarsons
46 Robert-Louis Stevenson Avenue
Westbourne
Bournemouth
Dorset BH4 8EJ

The publishers regret that they can enter into no corre-
spondence upon this matter.

## Editor's note

Readers may wish to read this title in conjunction with the
following Osprey titles:

MAA 24 *The Panzer Divisions*
New Vanguard 1 *King Tiger Heavy Tank*
New Vanguard 5 *Tiger 1 Heavy Tank*
New Vanguard 19 *Stug III*
New Vanguard 22 *Panther Variants 1942-45*

# GERMAN FLAME-THROWERS 1941-1945

# DESIGN LIMITATIONS

An article entitled *Flammenwerfer in Panzerkampfwagen*, written by Oberstleutnant Dr.-Ing. Olbrich of the Heeres Wa Prüf 6 (Army Automotive Design Department), was published in June 1939. As related by the following excerpts, Olbrich's article provides a unique insight into the complex factors governing the design of flamethrowing tanks.

Olbrich credited the first use of flamethrowers in tanks to the Italians during their campaign in Abyssinia in 1936. A traversable flamethrower was installed in the Ansaldo C.V.33 Carri-Fiammi light tank, replacing the machine gun (MG). The flame oil container was towed behind the tank on a single axle trailer.

A flamethrower operates simply by applying pressure to the flame oil, thereby forcing a stream of flame oil to spray out of a uniquely shaped nozzle. Pressure could be applied to the flame oil in one of three ways:

1. Utilising gravity (mounting the fuel tank above the nozzle)
2. Using a cylinder of compressed gas
3. Using a charging pump

The Germans only considered the last two methods, compressed gas or a charging pump, as practical for flamethrowers installed in tanks.

In addition to pressure applied to the fluid, many interrelated factors affected the range of the weapons: 1. The shape and cross-sectional area of the nozzle; 2. The flowrate through the nozzle; 3. The comparative size of the delivery tube and the nozzle; 4. Air resistance, windspeed and direction; 5. How well the fluid stream remains intact from the time it leaves the nozzle until it hits the ground; 6. The angle of elevation of the nozzle when the fluid is released; 7. The pressure losses within the flamethrower fuel delivery system from the storage tank to the nozzle.

Pressure losses within the system could reduce range to the extent that the flamethrower was worthless as a weapon. Therefore, the length of the fuel delivery lines had to be kept short by mounting the large pressurised gas cylinders or a charging pump close to the nozzle. In an attempt to minimise pressure losses, the Germans placed the fuel storage and delivery system inside the tank in close proximity to the crew. The amount of pressure applied was also restricted by the ability to completely seal the gaskets and couplings in the fuel delivery system. In 1939, the Germans thought that high pressure – over about 8 atmospheres – in the fighting compartment would give the crew the perception that it was unsafe.

In theory, as system pressure is increased, the range of the flamethrower should correspondingly increase. But as fluid is discharged at higher pressures, the fluid velocity increases and is counteracted by an increase in air resistance. Tests conducted by the Germans proved that no matter how much higher pressure was increased there was a maximum range associated with each nozzle size.

By 1939, the Germans had determined through experiments that, at the optimum pressure and no wind, ignited flame oil could be propelled out to a range of 80 metres. Sixty or seventy litres of fuel had to be expended per spurt in order to achieve this range. Shorter ranges were easily achieved with a more economical expenditure of fuel.

It was also observed that crosswinds greatly hindered any attempts to propel streams of burning oil to ranges in excess of 50 m. Crosswinds did not substantially effect ranges under 30 m. The speed of a tank also reduced flamethrower range. When flame oil is sprayed from a moving tank the increase in air resistance will cause the range to decrease. Therefore, targets within the 'specification' range could not be effectively engaged by tanks charging at high speed. The optimum range for an effective flamethrowing weapon was determined by careful evaluation of all of these factors. Assuming a fixed fuel capacity, the choices were limited to (1) Flammpanzer (flamethrower tanks) that could deliver many bursts at shorter ranges (up to 40 m) or (2) Flammpanzer that could only deliver a few bursts at long ranges (50-80 m).

As in the Italian design, the additional flame oil needed for a longer range flamethrower could be transported in a trailer. But towing a trailer greatly restricted the manoeuvrability and turning radius of a tank. In order to prevent loss of the trailer, the tanks had to slow down or were impeded from crossing trenches and other obstacles.

The Germans determined that there was no loss in combat effectiveness for flamethrower tanks with smaller, internal flame oil cells when compared to those with larger, towed flame oil cells. An adequate flame oil supply could be carried inside the tank to achieve the combat objectives at shorter ranges. From their first attempts in 1939, German engineers were capable of designing and installing longer range flamethrowers in their Flammpanzern. After evaluating all of the perti-nent factors, they decided in favour of increased mobility instead of longer range.

# PANZER I

The first attempt at mounting a flamethrower in a German tank was not the result of an engineering design process. It simply occurred as a field expe-dient in Spain. Crews were disappointed by the inherent inaccuracy of MGs fired from tanks charging into action. Therefore, it was suggested that a flamethrower would be a more suitable weapon. The few known details on this initial attempt are included in a report to the German General Staff on the Spanish Civil War dated 30 March 1939. As revealed in this report, the nozzle from the kleine Flammenwerfer (small back-pack flamethrower) could be easily fastened into the right-hand, MG mount in the Pz.Kpfw.I turret. The report stated that a flamethrower with a longer range was desired due to relatively high crew casualties.

Based on experiences in Spain from the 'volun-teers' of Panzer-Regiment 6 and the success of the Italians with their C.V.33 Carri-Fiammi, Panzer-Regiment 5 repeated the experiment in North

*Panzer Regiment 5 created these makeshift Panzerkampfwagen I (Flamm) by installing a back-pack flamethrower in place of one of the MGs in the turrets of some Pz.Kpfw.I Ausf.As. These Flammpanzers attempted to dislodge the defenders from their concrete bunkers around the perimeter of Tobruk.*

Africa. A back-pack kleine Flammenwerfer borrowed from the Pioniere (combat engineers) was again installed in the turret of a Pz.Kpfw.I, this time an Ausf.A. These tank mounted flamethrowers were used in an attempt to smoke out the occupants of the concrete emplacements in the Tobruk perimeter defences.

# PANZER II (F) (SD.KFZ.122)

### Description and Specifications

The first Flammpanzer to be specifically designed as such was officially known as the Panzerflammwagen (Sd.Kfz.122), or Panzerkampfwagen (F) (Sd.Kfz.122). Later the designation was altered to the now familiar Panzerkampfwagen II (Flamm) (Sd.Kfz.122).

In response to their proposal, the Heeres Waffenamt (Army Ordnance Department) had received authorisation on 21 January 1939 from Inspektorate 6 to design and develop an experimental 0-Serie of Flammpanzer. Wa Prüf 6 (the automotive design office of the Heeres Waffenamt) created a specification and contracted with MAN, Nürnberg to design the chassis, and Daimler-Benz, Berlin-Marienfelde to design the turret and superstructure. The resulting design was a tank

*The Panzerkampfwagen II (F) was converted from the Panzerkampfwagen II Ausf.D/E. A new small turret was fitted with a single ball-mounted MG34. To provide a good view of the flamethrowers, the turret had vision blocks of the type normally used for the driver. These large glass blocks were protected by a hinged visor on each of the forward facing sides of the turret. The Panzerkampfwagen II Ausf.D may be identified by its dry pin steel tracks. (US Official)*

mounting two Flammenwerfer nozzles in traversable Spritzköpfe (spray heads) located at the front of each fender. These separately operated Spritzköpfe were traversable through 180°, from a 9 o'clock through a 3 o'clock position. Each of the Flammenwerfer had a separate flame oil container holding 160 litres, sufficient for 80 bursts of 2-3 seconds duration. Four cylinders filled with compressed nitrogen provided the propulsion force. Compressed acetylene was used to ignite the flame oil.

An MG34 in the turret was mounted in a traversable ball mount with an elevation arc from -10° to +20°. This MG was sighted with a KZF2 gunsight registered at a range of 200 m. A total of 1,800 rounds of belted ammunition were carried in 12 bags each containing 150 rounds of SmK (armour piercing) ammunition.

A crew of three manned this 12 ton Flammpanzer. The commander also served as the main gunner for the MG and flamethrowers. A radio operator seated at the right front manned the Funkgerät 2 radio receiver set and also served as a second gunner for the flamethrowers. The driver was located in the left front.

Armour protection consisted of 30 mm plates on the front and 14.5 mm plates for the sides and rear. This armour provided effective protection

| Table I: Pz.Kpfw.II (F) Specifications |
| --- |
| Length: *4.90 m* |
| Width: *2.40 m* |
| Height: *1.85 m* |
| Ground clearance: *0.34 m* |
| Weight (combat loaded): *12 t* |
| Fuel capacity: *200 litres* |
| Max. speed: *55 km/h* |
| Cruising speed (on roads): *40 km/h* |
| Cross-country speed: *20 km/h* |
| Range (on roads): *250 km* |
| Range (cross-country): *125 km* |
| Max. gradient: *30°* |
| Step climbing ability: *0.42 m* |
| Trench crossing ability: *1.70 m* |
| Fording depth: *0.90 m* |
| Ground pressure: *0.85 kg/cm2* |
| Power-to-weight ratio: *11.7 metric hp/ton* |

against all calibres of anti-tank weapons up to 25 mm at ranges over 600 m. The 14.5 mm thick plates were adequate to provide protection against armour-piercing rounds fired from small arms (8 mm and less) at all ranges.

The La.S.138 chassis designed by MAN for the Pz.Kpfw.II Ausf.D was selected for the Flammpanzer. Power was provided by a six-cylinder, water-cooled, 6.2 litre, Maybach HL 62 TRM petrol engine delivering 140 metric hp at 2,600 rpm. A semi-automatic, seven-speed Maybach SRG 14 479 transmission transferred the power forward through the clutch-steering unit and final drives to the drive sprockets propelling the tracks. This chassis was one of the first with torsion bar suspension for the four large diameter road wheels mounted on each side.

## Production

Starting in April 1939, continuing through August 1939, 46 La.S.138 chassis, assembled in automotive running order by MAN, were set aside for mounting the Flammpanzer superstructure and turret. The Versuchsfahrzeug (trial vehicle) with a soft-steel superstructure was completed in July 1939. Final assembly of complete Flammpanzer with superstructure and turrets commenced at Wegmann & Co, Kassel, in January 1940. In March 1940, 43 Pz.Kpfw.II Ausf.D were returned by the troops for conversion as Flammpanzer. As ordered on 8 March 1940, ten Pz.Kpfw.II Ausf.D from the 7.Panzer-Division and 20 from the 8.Panzer-Division were returned to the ordnance depot at Magdeburg. After assembly of the first 20, a factory recall was issued in April 1940 to return all previously completed Flammpanzer for modifications requested by the troops as a result of initial trials.

Assembly of acceptable Pz.Kpfw.II(F) (Sd.Kfz.122), 1.Serie La.S.138(F) (Fgst.Nr. 27001-27085 and 27801-27000) commenced in May 1940 and continued through October 1940. The monthly production figures reported by the acceptance inspectors adds to a total of 86. But an independent Waffenamt report stated that 87 Flammpanzer had been completed by October along with three additional superstructures. All of the initial order for 90 0-Serie superstructures and turrets had been completed, leaving three superstructures without chassis. Assembly of the last three Flammpanzer in the 0-Serie was delayed until February 1941, when three additional chassis were made available for conversion.

Before production of the initial series was well underway or tested in combat, orders had already been placed for a second series. On 8 March 1940, MAN reported that they were to be awarded an additional contract for 150 La.S.138 chassis and superstructures for Flammpanzer. These were to be delivered at the rate of 30 per month at the end of 1941. This 2.Serie La.S.138 was given Fgst.Nr. series 27101-27250. In August 1941, MAN reported that assembly of the 2.Serie had already commenced. In the interim it had been decided to complete only 90 of this series as Flammpanzer. The remaining 60 chassis were to be completed as normal Pz.Kpfw.II Ausf.D (2.Serie La.S.138 (2 cm)) tanks. By November 1941, this decision had been reversed and all 150 of the 2.Serie were to be completed as Flammpanzer.

On 20 December 1941, the Waffenamt was informed of the decision to use the 2.Serie chassis as mounts for self-propelled anti-tank guns. Production ceased in March 1942, after a total of only 62 Pz.Kpfw.II (F) (Sd.Kfz.122) Ausf.B, 2.Serie La.S.138(F) (Fgst.Nr. 27101-28250) had been completed. Including these 62 chassis, all 150 chassis from the 2.Serie were used as mounts for self-propelled 7.62 cm Pak.36(r) anti-tank guns.

## Organisation

On 1 March 1940, orders were cut to create the first Panzerflammabteilung (armoured flamethrower battalion, 'Panzerabteilung (F) 100' at the Panzertruppenschule in Wunsdorf with the following organisation:

Stab Pz.Abt.(F) (Battalion HQ) K.St.N.1110
  (*dated 28.2.40*)
Stbskp. Pz.Abt.(F) (HQ Co.) K.St.N.1151
  (*dated 28.2.40*)
Staffel Pz.Abt.(F) (Reserve) K.St.N.1179
  (*dated 28.2.40*)
3 Pz.Kp.(F) (Flamethrower Co.) K.St.N.1177
  (*dated 28.2.40*)
l.Kol.Pz.Abt.(F) (Supply Column) K.St.N.1188
  (*dated 28.2.40*)
l.Pz.Werkst.Zug (Workshop Platoon) K.St.N.1185
  (*dated 1.10.37*)

This initial order specified that the unit was to be trained and ready for combat operations on 10 July 1940. This reveals that the General Staff had no intention whatsoever of preparing an armoured

*Close-up of the Flammenwerfer-Spritz-köpfe (flamethrower spray head), projecting flame fuel. It was normal practice to douse the target in un-ignited flame oil before firing a burst of flame. The lubricated bearing track and associated drive sprocket of this Ausf.E chassis is clearly visible.*

flamethrower unit for the planned offensive in the West.

The headquarters for Pz.Abt.(F) 100 was officially established on 5 March 1940 followed by the three companies on 21 March 1940. The headquarters for a second Panzerabteilung (F), numbered 101, was established on 4 May 1940. During this same period the 1.Kompanie/Pz.Abt.(F) 101 was created on 26 April, the 2.Kompanie on 10 May and the 3.Kompanie on 1 May 1940.Only 16 Pz.Kpfw.II(F) were available on 19 June 1940. Even if a battalion had been completely trained and combat ready, there was insufficient equipment for them to have participated in the campaign in France in May and June 1940. To differentiate their vehicles from those of other units, each unit selected a symbol to stencil on their vehicles. The unit symbol for Pz.Abt.(F) 100 was a multi-coloured flame. The emblem for Pz.Abt.(F) 101 was crossed flamethrowers stenciled in light green paint on the turret rear.

Following adjustments to the organisation, by September 1940 each Panzerflammabteilung was to consist of one Stab (Headquarters), one Stabskompanie (Headquarters Company), three Panzerkompanien (F) (Armoured Flamethrower Companies), one Staffel (Reserve), one leichte Panzerflammkolonne (Light Supply Column), and one Panzer-Werkstattzug (Workshop Platoon).

Each Panzerkompanie (F), organised in accordance with K.St.N.1177 dated 1 February 1941, consisted of one Kompanietrupp (Kompanie Headquarters) with two Pz.Kpfw.II (2 cm) (Sd.Kfz.121), three Flammzuegen (Flamethrower Platoons) each with four Pz.Kpfw. (F) (Sd.Kfz.122), and one Waffenzug (Weapons Platoon) with five Pz.Kpfw.II (2 cm) (Sd.Kfz.121).

The Staffel Panzer Abteilung (F) organised in accordance with K.St.N.1179 dated 1 February 1941 held a reserve of two Pz.Kpfw.II (2 cm) (Sd.Kfz.121) and six Pz.Kpfw. (F) (Sd.Kfz.122). This reserve did not last long in practice. The Staffel for Pz.Abt.(F) 101 was absorbed into the three Panzerkompanie (F) and disbanded by the second day of action on 23 June 1941.

## Tactics

The manual for the Panzerflammabteilung (Panzerabteilung [F]) dated 1 September 1940 established the basic tactical doctrine and described combat capabilities as revealed in the following excerpts: 'Panzerflammwagen are close combat weapons for the Panzertruppe. They are to be utilised to expedite the destruction of the enemy in situations where success with other weapons is not achievable. Panzerflammwagen have a strong demoralising effect on the enemy.

'Panzerflammwagen are to use the Flammenwerfer to engage troops and combustible targets at close ranges (up to 30 m) and the machine gun to engage troop targets out to 400 m (the most effective range being 200 m). One load of fuel in the Pz.Kpfw.II(F) is sufficient for the two Flammenwerfer to each discharge 80 spurts of 2-3 seconds duration.

'The ignited oil destroys any enemy within the weapon's range and its demoralising effect drives the enemy out of cover to where they can be destroyed by other weapons. Attacks with flamethrowers are especially effective in flushing out nests of resistance in field fortifications, bunkers, buildings and woods.

'Targets are to be engaged by short bursts from one or both of the Flammenwerfer-Spritzkoepfe (flamethrower spray heads). When engaging opponents who are on flat terrain or not dug in, maximum effect can be achieved by discharging bursts at zero degrees elevation. The resulting spray will cover an area extending outward from about 10-20 m in front of the Flammpanzer. An area about 50 m wide can be covered by traversing the Spritzköpfe while spraying. In order to engage targets at higher or lower elevations, the Spritzkoepfe can be raised or lowered with a lever. Scattered targets can be engaged by simultaneously spraying with both Spritzkoepfe.

'Individual targets can most effectively be destroyed by firing when halted. Longer duration fires can be set by first spraying the area with cold oil to soak the target followed by a short burst of ignited flame oil. This method is recommended for engaging trenches, revetments, bunker emplacements, houses and log bunkers.

'The Panzerflammwagen are to advance under the covering fire of artillery or other normal armored units. At close range, covering fire is provided by the units own Pz.Kpfw.II platoons.

'For maximum effect, the entire Flammpanzerabteilung is to be sent into the attack with all three Panzerflammkompanien on a front no wider than 850 m. Only when the terrain restricts the deployment of the entire Panzerabteilung are company-sized units to be sent in. The Panzerabteilung is never to fight alone. It is to be attached to a Panzer-Division and only in rare cases to an Infanterie-Division'.

## Table 2: Operational Status Reports Pz. Abt.(F) 100

**Operational Status Reported on 22 July 1941**

|  | Pz.II | Pz.IIF | Pz.III | Pz.Bef. |
|---|---|---|---|---|
| Operational | 10 | 17 | 1 | 0 |
| In Repair | 8 | 14 | 3 | 1 |
| Total Loss | 6 | 11 | 1 | 0 |

**Operational Status Reported on 1 September 1941**

|  | Pz.II | Pz.IIF | Pz.III | Pz.Bef. |
|---|---|---|---|---|
| Operational | 16 | 15 | 2 | 0 |
| In Repair | 2 | 15 | 1 | 0 |
| Total Loss | 7 | 12 | 2 | 1 |

**Operational Status Reported on 30 September 1941**

|  | Pz.II | Pz.IIF | Pz.III | Pz.Bef. |
|---|---|---|---|---|
| Operational | 8 | 7 | 2 | 0 |
| In Repair | 7 | 20 | 1 | 0 |
| Total Loss | 10 | 15 | 2 | 1 |

**Operational Status Reported on 20 October 1941**

|  | Pz.II | Pz.IIF | Pz.III | Pz.Bef. |
|---|---|---|---|---|
| Operational | 11 | 7 | 2 | 0 |
| In Repair | 5 | 21 | 1 | 0 |
| Total Loss | 9 | 14 | 2 | 1 |

*Rare overhead view of a Panzerkampfwagen II (F) – based on the Panzerkampfwagen II Ausf.D – revealing the two Spritzköpfe and the shape of the turret. (Wegmann)*

However, in all cases it was to fight in co-ordination with other armoured units, concentrated to achieve decisive results. Normally other tanks and artillery were to engage and destroy any interfering enemy anti-tank weapons, artillery pieces or tanks. But, the Panzerflammwagen could take advantage of the heavy clouds of smoke created by the burning flame oil and use it as a screen to close within effective range or to take cover.

Not including delivery time, it took about an half an hour to refill each Panzerflammwagen with 320 litres of flame oil, the four cylinders with compressed nitrogen propellent, and the acetylene cylinder. If supply vehicles could reach the Flammpanzer, the entire company could be completely refilled in one hour.

## Combat Reports

Pz.Abt.(F) 100 was attached to the 18.Panzer-Division under the XLVII Panzer-Korps at the start of Operation 'Barbarossa' on 22 June 1941. Its initial strength reported on 18 June 1941 was 24 Pz.Kpfw.II, 42 Pz.Kpfw.II(F), five Pz.Kpfw. III(5 cm), and one gr.Pz.Bef.Wg.(Sd.Kfz.267). The operational status reports for Pz.Abt.(F) 100 in Table 2 reveal the operational strength and losses sustained during the heavy fighting in Russia during the summer and autumn of 1941.

On 5 November 1941, Pz.Flamm-Abt.100 was ordered to be pulled out of the front for rest and refitting. They were ordered to leave behind the serviceable tanks (11 Pz.Kpfw.II and two Pz.Kpfw.III) other than the Pz.Kpfw.II(F) and turn them over to the 18. Panzer-Division. After returning to their home base, on 22 December 1941, Pz.Abt.(F) 100 with its three companies was converted to a normal tank battalion and renamed as the I.Abteilung/Panzer-Regiment 100. Shortly thereafter on 5 February 1942, it was renamed as Panzer-Abteilung 'Grossdeutschland' and reorganised with three mittleren Kompanien (medium companies) each with ten Pz.Kpfw.IV. As part of the 'Grossdeutschland' Division, the unit returned to frontline action in Russia in the summer offensive of 1942.

*Right-hand rear of the Panzerkampfwagen II (F). A smoke candle dispenser is mounted on the rear plate, but is supplemented by three forward firing smoke candle launchers positioned behind the flame fuel tanks. (Wegmann)*

*This Panzerkampfwagen II (F) is from 2.Kompanie/Panzer Abteilung (F) 101. A detailed after-action report from the Eastern Front is described in the text.*

At the start of Operation 'Barbarossa' on 22 June 1941, Pz.Abt.(F) 101 was attached to Panzer-Gruppe 3. Its initial strength consisted of 25 Pz.Kpfw.II, 42 Pz.Kpfw.II(F), five Pz.Kpfw.III(5 cm), and one gr.Pz.Bef.Wg.(Sd.Kfz.267).

The following rare after-action report reveals how Pz.Abt.(F) 101 actually employed their Panzerflammwagen in an engagement on 26 August 1941 while attached to the 7.Panzer-Division: 'Having attacked across the Lojnja River by Bolotina, the enemy held an area approximately two kilometres wide and two kilometres deep. The I.Batallion/Schützen-Regiment 7 was to attack and restore the original defence line along the river. They were to be supported by Pz.Abt.(F) 101 on the left and Panzer-Regiment 25 on the right.

'Pz.Abt.(F) 101 started to advance at 0600 hours, 3.Kompanie on the right, 2.Kompanie on the left, with the 1.Kompanie following the 2.Kompanie. The initial attack on a wide front was disrupted by the terrain. The companies were forced to cross several deep gullies in single file which succeeded without delaying the advance.

'Even though only small arms fire had been received, it was expected that the enemy possessed anti-tank guns and supporting heavy weapons. The enemy infantry were reported to be hiding in a sector covered with brush in front of a woods. A deep gully located on the left flank couldn't be negotiated by tanks.

'Pz.Abt.(F) 101, advancing toward the woods to attack the brush covered sector, were not opposed by other than artillery fire. As it turned out, the woods were impenetrable to tanks. The commander tried to direct the unit around the left of the

| Table 3: Operational Status Reported on 8 November 1941, Pz. Abt. (F) 101 | | | | |
|---|---|---|---|---|
| | *Pz.II* | *Pz.IIF* | *Pz.III* | *Pz.Bef.* |
| Operational | 6 | 5 | 2 | 0 |
| In Repair | 12 | 20 | 1 | 0 |
| Total Loss | 7 | 17 | 2 | 1 |

woods. This attempt was aborted after encountering the deep gully and boggy terrain.

'In the meantime, the German infantry attacked toward the woods and were opposed by machine gun and rifle fire. The commander turned Pz.Abt.(F) 101 toward the south along the west edge of the woods and brushland. The 3.Kompanie and a section of two Pz.Kpfw.III (5 cm) was at the point with the 2.Kompanie eche-

*Panzerkampfwagen II (F) destroyed during the advance into Russia in July 1941. This photograph gives a rare view of the front of a Panzerkampfwagen II (F). (Bundesarchiv)*

loned to the left. The 1.Kompanie was at first held in reserve in a gully to the west of the brush land. A second section of two Pz.Kpfw.III (5 cm) were ordered to scout the wood line along the east edge of the woods.

'The 2. and 3. Kompanie started to burn out the brushland. It turned out that the area was heavily occupied by Russian infantry. The attack could only be conducted in steps since the Russians crawled into their holes and German infantry weren't immediately available to flush them out. However, the enemy were prevented from firing on our advancing infantry who quickly gained ground, some elements reaching the brush land. Then the enemy was systematically smoked out. The first prisoners, with panic stricken, terrified expressions on their faces, were forced out. Brush-pile after brush-pile was then burnt out. Several Russians still fired from hidden positions, so that a second pass through the area was necessary.

'The 1.Kompanie advanced along the eastern edge of the woods, burning out any remaining enemy infantry. Enemy resistance was brought to

an end after sending in a Flammpanzer platoon of the 2.Kompanie. At the same time, the 3.Kompanie combed through the open area and cornfields. Many enemy infantry were also discovered dug-in in this sector. The 2.Kompanie was also sent in and cleaned out the rest of the area.

'In the meantime, the German infantry reached their objectives and dug-in. At 1100 hours, Pz.Abt.(F) 101 started back to their original assembly area after observing Panzer-Regiment 25 pull out and ensuring that the infantry could hold the positions without their support.

'About 1230 hours, a radio message received from the I.Batallion/Schützen-Regiment 7 stated that the battalion was under attack from the front, flanks and rear. The 1.Kompanie/Panzer-Abteilung (F) 101 was sent to their relief. Upon arriving, the infantry commander informed them that the situation had cleared up and the Flammkompanie was no longer needed. As a precaution, the 1.Kompanie was left at the front until 1900 hours. Equipment definitely destroyed by Pz.Abt.(F) 101 amounted to several light machine

guns, 11 heavy machine guns, one mortar, two cars, three trucks, and one tank. Pz.Abt.(F) 101 claimed probable destruction of a heavy tank and two artillery pieces. Forty prisoners were turned over to the infantry. About 100 to 150 enemy infantry were killed by the flamethrowers and machine gun gun fire. Pz.Abt.(F) 101 did not suffer any losses in men or material.'

The operational status report for Pz.Abt.(F) 101 in Table 3 reveals their operational strength and the losses sustained during the heavy fighting in Russia during the summer and autumn of 1941.

After being pulled out of the front and returned to their home base, on 10 December 1941, Pz.Abt.(F) 101 with its three companies were disbanded and used in the creation of Panzer-Regiment 24. Outfitted as a normal Panzer-Regiment, as part of the 24.Panzer-Division, the unit returned to the Eastern Front to take part in the summer offensives of 1942.

# PANZER B2 (F)

On 26 May 1941, Flammenwerferwagen were briefly discussed in a meeting with Hitler. Photographs were shown of the 85 Pz.Kpfw.II

*The first series of 24 Panzerkampfwagen B2 (F) were converted in time for 'Barbarossa' in 22 June 1941. Captured French Heavy tanks were equipped with the same flamethrower system as the Pz.Kpfw.II (F), which used compressed nitrogen as the propellant. The hull-mounted 75 mm gun was removed and replaced by a Flammenwerfer-Spritzköpf (flamethrower spray head) similar to those used on the Pz.Kpfw.I (F). These Panzerkampfwagen B2 (F) served with Panzerabteilung (F) 102. (Thomas Jung)*

(Flammenwerfer) that were already available with the troops. In addition, progress on conversion of captured Pz.Kpfw.B2 (known to the French as the Char B1bis) with flamethrowers was discussed. Hitler responded to the report that two companies each with 12 B2 Flamm-Wagen were projected to be available by 20 June 1941 with the remark that this deadline was satisfactory.

This initial series of 24 Pz.Kpfw.B2 (F) were equipped with the same flamethrower system as the Pz.Kpfw.II (F) utilising compressed nitrogen as the propellant. After removing the 75 mm gun that had been mounted in the right front of the tank a Flammenwerfer-Spritzköpf (flamethrower spray head) was mounted in the evacuated position.

All 24 Pz.Kpfw.B2 (F) were issued to Panzerabteilung (F) 102. This unit was created on 20 June 1941 with two schwere Flamm-Kompanie organised in accordance with K.St.N.1176 dated

The final series of Panzerkampfwagen B2 (F) had a new ball-mounted flame projector. The fighting compartment was extended and a driver-type vision block with an armoured visor provided for the operator. This photograph shows the ball mount and projector disassembled. (Tank Museum)

### Table 4: Pz.Kpfw.B2 (F) Specifications

Length: *6.86 m*
Width: *2.52 m*
Height: *2.88 m*
Ground clearance: *0.45 m*
Weight (combat loaded): *32 t*
Fuel capacity: *400 litres*
Max. speed: *28 km/h*
Cruising speed (on roads): *12.5 km/h*
Range (on roads): *140 km*
Range (cross-country): *100 km*
Fording depth: *0.72 m*
Ground pressure: *0.85 kg/cm2*
Power-to-weight ratio: *9.4 metric hp/ton*

30 May 1941. At the time they were created, in addition to the 12 Pz.Kpfw.B2 (F), each company had three normal Pz.Kpfw.B1 with 75 mm guns.

Pz.Abt.(F) 102 arrived at the front on the 23rd of June 1941, the day after the start of Operation 'Barbarossa'. Under Armee-Oberkommando 17, Pz.Abt.(F) 102 was assigned to the 24.Infanterie-Division on 24 June and the 296.Infanterie-Division on 26 June to support the attacks on the border fortress of 'Wielki Dzial'. On 24 June, Pz.Abt.(F) 102 were reported to have successfully reduced a bunker. Some of the Russians had pulled back into field emplacements.

On 29 June by 1300 hours, the commander of the 296.Infanterie-Division reported that 'Wielki Dzial' had been captured. The combat report from the II./Infanterie-Regiment 520 provides details on the participation of Pz.Abt.(F) 102: 'During the evening of 28 June, Pz.Abt.(F) 102 pulled forward into their assigned assembly area.

In response to the loud noise from the tank motors the opponent opened lively fire with guns and machine guns but didn't hit anyone.

'After a delay to let the fog clear, at 0555 hours on 29 June, the action was opened by 88 mm Flak guns firing directly at the embrasures of the bunkers. Fire from the 88s was continued to 0704 during which time it was observed that most of

Detail of the flame projector on the final series of Panzerkampfwagen B2 (F). (Tank Museum)

*This Panzerkampfwagen B2 (F) was knocked out in Osterbeck near Arnhem, Holland, towards the end of September 1944. A old style smoke candle discharger was fitted to the side of the turret by the unit. (Bundesarchiv)*

the embrasures had been hit and silenced.

'Responding to a green flare, the Flammpanzer of Pz.Abt.(F) 102 attacked at 0705 hours. The Infanterie-Pioniere following directly behind the Flammpanzer were assigned the objective of placing explosive charges on the bunkers. When several of the bunkers again opened fire, some of the Pioniere sought temporary shelter in the anti-tank ditch. Covering fire was provided by the 88 mm Flak guns and other heavy weapons. Bunkers No. 1 through 4 were suppressed by the Flammpanzer. The Infanterie-Pioniere storm troops reached the bunkers and began to place and detonate their explosive charges.

'Bunkers No.1, 2 and 4 damaged by hits from the 88s could only fire infrequently fire. The Flammpanzer were able to almost completely hold

them in check. The crews in the bunkers tenaciously resisted in spite of the damage. Two Flammpanzer were hit by 75 mm guns firing from Bunker No.3a. Both Flammpanzer caught fire and their crews evacuated. Three slightly wounded crew members were rescued under enemy fire by the brave actions of Sanitäts-Unteroffizier Kannengiesser. The Flammenwerfer did not damage the bunkers. The flame oil did not penetrate through the ball mounts in the embrasures. Some of the bunkers continued to fire after being engaged by the Flammpanzer.'

On 30 June 1941, Pz.Abt.(F) 102 was reassigned directly under the command of Armee-Oberkommando 17. By 27 July 1941, Pz.Abt.(F) 102 had been ordered to be disbanded. Further development of the tank mounted flamethrowers was ordered to continue, again utilising the Pz.Kpfw.Renault B2 (F). The new specifications were for a Flammenwerfer with pressure supplied by a pump driven by a J10-Motor. It was to be

capable of spraying out to a range of 40-45 m and carry sufficient flame oil for 200 bursts. The flamethrower was still mounted beside the driver in place of the dismounted 7.5 cm gun. Daimler-Benz designed the armour protection modifications, Wegmann the mounting, and Koebe the flamethrower. The flame oil was carried in a large armoured container fitted to the rear of the hull.

In addition to the flamethrower in the hull, a 47 mm gun and a MG were mounted in the turret. A crew of four manned this 32 ton Flammpanzer. Armour protection on the hull consisted of 40 to 60 mm plates on the front and 60 mm plates on the sides and 55 mm plates on the rear. The cast armour on the turret was 55 mm thick on the front and 45 mm thick on the sides and rear. Power was provided by a six-cylinder, water-cooled, 16.94 litre, Renault petrol engine delivering 300 hp (metric) at 1,900 rpm. A five-speed transmission transferred the power through the controlled-differential steering unit and final drives to the drive sprockets propelling the tracks.

The planned production schedule reported on 3 December 1941 was for a single series, ten to be completed in December 1941 and a further ten in January 1942. The Waffenamt reported accepting a total of 20 Pz.Kpfw.B2 (Flamm) as follows: five in November 1941, three in December 1941, three

in March 1942, two in April, three in May and four in June 1942. Further production statistics were not reported beyond June 1942 by the Waffenamt in Berlin since the responsibility for conversions to Flammwagen B2 was transferred to an ordnance depot in France.

As revealed by operational status reports, in total there were at least 60 Pz.Kpfw.B2 (Fl) equipped with the newly designed pump driven flamethrower system. As reported on 31 May 1943, they were distributed to the following units: Panzer-Kompanie 223 with 16 Pz.Kpfw.B2 of which 12 were Pz.Kpfw.B2 (Fl) on the Eastern Front, Panzer-Brigade 100 with 34 Pz.Kpfw.B2 of which 24 were Pz.Kpfw.B2 (Fl) and Panzer-Abteilung 213 with 36 Pz.Kpfw.B2 of which ten were Pz.Kpfw.B2 (Fl) in the West, and SS 'Prinz Eugen' with 17 Pz.Kpfw.B2 of which an unknown number were Pz.Kpfw.B2 (Fl) in Yugoslavia.

# PANZER III (Fl) (SD.KFZ.141/3)

### Description and Specifications

The flamethrower system developed for the Pz.Kpfw.B2 (Fl) was subsequently mounted in the

Pz.Kpfw.III turret. The turret could be continuously traversed through 360° by installing a packing box connection in the flame oil delivery pipe. The flamethrower and co-axially mounted MG34 could be elevated through an arc from minus -10/+20°. There was no sighting device other than a vane sight positioned in front of the forward view port in the commander's cupola. Two containers inside the hull held 1020 litres of flame oil.

A range of 50 m could be achieved with cold flame oil (60 m when ignited) by 15 to 17 atmospheres of pressure provided by the Koebe pump delivered at a flow rate of 7.8 litres/sec. The Koebe pump was driven by a two-stroke, 28 metric hp, Auto-Union ZW 1101 (DKW) engine running off a mixture of oil and petrol. The flame oil was ignited using electric 'Smitskerzen' (Smits' glow plug).

A second MG34 was mounted in a traversable ball mount in the superstructure front plate with an elevation arc from -10°/+20°. This ball-mounted MG was aimed using a KZF2 gunsight

registered at a range of 200 m. Some 3,750 rounds of belted ammunition were carried for the MGs in bags each containing 150 rounds of SmK (armour piercing) ammunition.

A crew of three manned this 23.8 ton Flammpanzer. The commander (also served as the gunner for the flamethrower and the turret-mounted MG). A radio operator seated at the right front manned the Funkgerät 5 radio transmitter and receiver set and also served as a gunner for the ball-mounted MG. The driver was located in the left front.

Armour protection for the chassis consisted of 30 plus 50 mm plates on the hull front, 20 plus 50 mm plates on the driver's front plate, 30 mm plates on the hull sides and 50 mm plates for the hull rear. The turret had 20 plus 50 mm plates for the gun mantle and 30 mm plates for the sides and rear. The frontal armour was adequately

*A 1:76 scale 4-view drawing of the*
*Panzerkampfwagen III (Fl) (Author)*

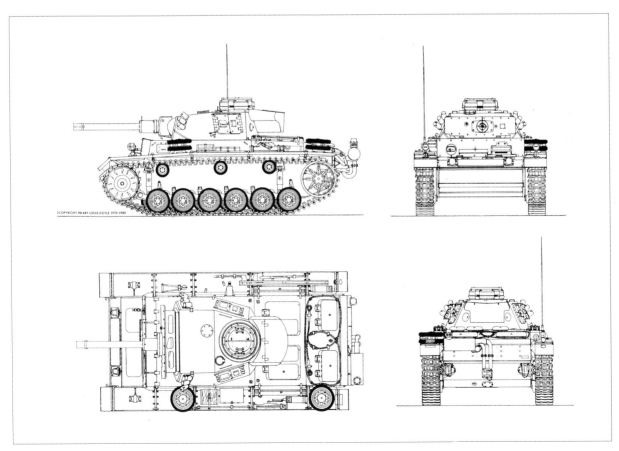

## Table 5: Pz.Kpfw.III (Fl) Operational Status Reports for 1943

|  | 31 Mar | 30 Apr | 31 May | 30 Jun | 31 Jul | 31 Aug | 30 Sep | 31 Oct | 30 Nov | 31 Dec |
|---|---|---|---|---|---|---|---|---|---|---|
| **In Russia:** | | | | | | | | | | |
| 1.Pz.Div. |  |  |  |  |  |  |  | 7 | 6 | 0 |
| 6.Pz.Div. | 15 | 15 | 14 | 14 | 13 | 7 | 4 | 4 | 3 | 3 |
| 11.Pz.Div. |  | 3 | 13 | 13 | 13 | 8 | 8 | 5 | 5 | 0 |
| 14.Pz.Div. |  |  |  |  |  |  |  | 7 | 7 | 5 |
| 24.Pz.Div. |  |  |  |  |  |  |  | 14 | 13 | 13 |
| Grossdeutschland | 27 | 24 | 14 | 14 | 12 | 11 | 10 | 7 | 0 | 0 |
| **In Italy:** | | | | | | | | | | |
| 16.Pz.Div. |  | 7 | 7 | 7 | 7 | 7 | 2 | 2 | 2 | 0 |
| 26.Pz.Div. |  |  |  |  | 14 | 14 | 14 | 14 | 14 | 11 |
| Operational: | 10 | 31 | 34 | 39 | 29 | 33 | 19 | 38 | 23 | 15 |
| In Repair: | 32 | 18 | 14 | 9 | 30 | 14 | 19 | 22 | 27 | 17 |
| Total: | 42 | 49 | 48 | 48 | 59 | 47 | 38 | 60 | 50 | 32 |
| Monthly Losses: | 1 | 0 | 1 | 0 | 3 | 12 | 9 | 6 | 10 | 18 |

designed to protect against penetration by the Russian 76 mm or American 75 mm tank guns at normal combat ranges. A total of five fire extinguishers were carried; three on the inside and two on the outside.

Power was provided by a twelve-cylinder, water-cooled, 12 litre, Maybach HL 120 TRM petrol engine delivering 265 bhp (metric) at 2,600 rpm. A synchronised, six-speed Zahnradfabrik SSG 77 transmission transferred the power forward through the planetary gear steering unit and final drives to the drive sprockets propelling the tracks. Each of the six road wheels mounted on each side were sprung by independent torsion bar suspension.

## Production

One hundred chassis (with Fgst.Nr. 77609-77708) were completed in automotive running order by the firm of Miag in Braunsweig. Impressive in number, these vehicles were delivered to Wegmann in Kassel for installation of the flamethrower assembly and mounting the turret. The production schedule had called for 20 to be completed in January, 45 in February and 35 in March 1943. Following a one month delay, 65 Panzerflammwagen (Sd.Kfz.141) were accepted by Waffenamt inspectors in February, 34 in March and the last one in April 1943. It was not until

later that the official designation was changed to Pz.Kpfw.III (Fl) (Sd.Kfz.141/3).

## Organisation and Combat Reports

Previously Flammpanzer were organised as independent army battalions that were only attached to higher headquarters. But the Pz.Kpfw.III (Fl) was issued to platoons incorporated as an organic part of a normal Panzer-Abteilung Stabskompanie. Officially known as a Panzer-Flamm-Zug, it was organised in accordance with K.St.N.1190 dated 25 January 1943 with seven 'Panzerflammwagen (Sd.Kfz.141)'.

A report dated 5 May 1941 stated that all 100 Panzerflammwagen had been issued as follows: 28 to Division 'Grossdeutschland', 15 to the 6. Panzer-Division, 14 to the 1.Panzer-Division, 14 to the 24. Panzer-Division, 14 to the 26.Panzer-Division, seven to the 14.Panzer-Division, seven to the 16. Panzer-Division, and a single vehicle to Schule Wunsdorf.

Only seven of the 14 issued to the 1.Panzer-Division accompanied the unit to Russia. The other seven were turned over to the Ersatzheer (reserve army) by 31 October 1943 and retained at the home station. Thirteen of the 28 issued to 'Grossdeutschland' were re-issued to the 11. Panzer-Division. The status reports for 1943 in Table 5 reveal the number available with each unit

and the loss rate of Pz.Kpfw.III (Fl) in action at the front.

An exceptionally rare combat report recorded the action of the 1.Flamm-Kompanie/Panzer-Regiment 26 near Mozzagrogna, Italy on 28 November 1943. This outfit was unique in that the Panzer-Flamm-Zug attached to each Panzer-Abteilung of Panzer-Regiment 26 was expanded into a company-sized unit. This was achieved by adding platoons of Sturmhaubitze and Sturmgeschütze confiscated from the Italians to create the 'Flamm-Kompanie'. This report stated that for the first time Flammpanzer in Panzer-Regiment 26 had gone into action with favourable results: 'During the evening of 27 November, the enemy penetrated the main battle line and captured the town of Mozzagrogna. Having been attached to the 65 Infanterie-Division, the 1.Flamm-Kompanie together with the 1.Aufklärung-Schwadron (1st recon squadron) were to attack at 0500 toward Mozzagrogna with the objective of throwing the enemy out of the

*A Panzerkampfwagen III (Fl) being put through its paces during a training exercise. The flame and smoke certainly attracted a lot of attention. These Panzerkampfwagen III (Fl) were built in 1943. They were based on the Panzerkampfwagen III Ausf.M which featured deep wading seals and a raised exhaust with an non-return valve. (US Official)*

town and restoring the main battle line. The combat orders for the company declared in part: "Together with 1.Aufklärung-Schwadron, the town is to be retaken while it is still dark before enemy air force activity begins. To avoid losses, the tanks are to be pulled back under cover of darkness to the ravine by Mozzagrogna."

'At the start of the counter-attack the combat strength of the 1.Flamm-Kompanie with an attached platoon from the 7.Panzer-Kompanie was five Flamm-Panzer, four Pz.Kpfw.IV (7.5 cm Kw.K.40 L/48), one Pz.Kpfw.IV (7.5 cm Kw.K. L/24), three Sturmhaubitze (10.5 cm) (ital.), and three Sturmgeschütze (7.5 cm) (ital.).

'After brief instructions on co-operation with

*The Flame projector was designed to eliminate bunkers at*
*a relatively short range. (US Official).*

tanks were given to the Aufklärung-Schwadron, at about 0500 the 1.Flamm-Kompanie started to counter-attack. All combat elements of the company reached the entrance to the town at about 0600. Here the combined Flammpanzer and gun-armed armoured vehicles began to attack.

'The attack surprised the opponent resulting in the capture of the town by about 0730 hours. Co-operation with the Aufklaerung-Schwadron left much to be desired. Their individual sections, intended for employment as close defence for the tanks, followed behind, bunched together. It was thereby unpreventable that losses occurred to the infantry. The commander of a Flammpanzer, Feldwebel Hoffmann, was shot in the head and killed during an attack against a field fortification which had been hastily erected in the town.

'An artillery hit broke the track and damaged the drive sprocket of Feldwebel Bock's Flammpanzer, leaving it immobilised. This incident was not noticed since Feldwebel Bock had advanced as the head of his section. His radio message, sent before dismounting, went unheard.

*The crew of '411' have camouflaged their Panzerkampfwagen III (Fl) by daubing olivgrün (Dark olive green) and/or rotbraun (Dark chocolate brown) paste over the base coat of dunkelgelb (Tan). (US Official)*

This was caused by several radio sets being knocked out of service by shock waves from closely detonating shells and bombs.

'To prevent congestion during the return trip vehicles were ordered to return singly and spaced far apart to the old assembly area. This fact aided in explaining why at first the absence of the Flammpanzer of Feldwebel Bock was not noticed by any member of the company.

'About an hour after the withdrawal of the company, the British brought up reinforcements and enemy fighter-bombers crossed above the town. The Aufklärung-Schwadron partially evacuated the town. After being fired at by a machine gun and infantry while attempting to repair the track, Feldwebel Bock knew that he had to abandon the Flammpanzer and blew it up. He withdrew with his crew until he met several soldiers from the Aufklärung-Schwadron. He and his crew then took part as infantry in the fight until the main battle line was again in our hands. The crew arrived back at the company position at about 1700.

'The 1.Flamm-Kompanie brought in an English captain and 13 Indian soldiers as prisoners. The enemy losses in dead and wounded, partly through flame-thrower action, partly by gunfire,

*Also featured as a cutaway, this Panzerkampfwagen III (Fl), tactical number 'F24', and another Panzerkampfwagen III (Fl), tactical number 'F23', were captured in Italy. This particular vehicle was shipped to Aberdeen Proving Grounds, USA, where it was on display for many years. It is currently housed in the Koblenz Musuem, Germany. (US Official)*

were at least as high. During the return trip in daylight, the tanks were spotted and decimated by repeated enemy bombing attacks. Four Flammpanzer, four Pz.Kpfw.IV, two Sturmhaubitze and three Sturmgeschütze were lightly damaged. Only one Pz.Kpfw.IV (L/24) and one Sturmhaubitze remained fully operational. The damaged Panzers were towed away from the enemy lines.'

A second rare combat report recorded the counter-attack by the 2.Flamm-Kompanie/Panzer-Regiment 26 and Oberleutnant Ruckdeschel on 16 December 1943: 'At 0300 hours, the 2.Flamm-Kompanie under the command of Leutnant Tag with five Flammpanzer III and two Sturmhaubitze (10.5 cm) (ital.) started to counter-attack, advancing behind the gun-armed tank of Oberleutnant Ruckdeschel. Very strong enemy resistance consisting mainly of heavy machine gun fire was encountered after crossing the front line along the Ortona to Orsogna road. Shortly thereafter, a

major bombardment of enemy artillery fell along and on both sides of the road.

'Initially advancing along the road, the 2.Flamm-Kompanie supported the advance of the Fallschirmjäger (airborne infantry) with covering machine gun fire. After recognising the main nests of enemy resistance, the armoured vehicles pulled off the road to the left. It was possible for the Flammpanzer to advance cross-country in this area. Under covering fire provided by the Sturmhaubitze, the Flammwagen could smoke out a large number of enemy machine gun and infantry positions. The enemy resistance broke as a result of tremendous losses.

'Concentrated gun fire from the Sturmhaubitze and supporting machine gun fire from all the Panzers inflicted bloody losses on the enemy.

'A Flammwagen succeeded in destroying an enemy tank. The type of tank could not be determined in the darkness. The Flammwagen had adroitly crept up on the enemy tank that was hidden under cover of a straw stack and set it on fire with several spurts from the flamethrower.

'In the meantime, enemy action against the leading Panzers had greatly increased by the addition of several anti-tank weapons. In addition, the road had been mined by the opponent. This position couldn't be bypassed because of the nature of

the terrain. This delay was exploited by the Flammpanzer. They renewed the search for enemy infantry in the immediate area and began to destroy or drive them out with machine gun fire and spurts of flame oil.

'During this battle, the Flammpanzer in the company discharged more than 150 spurts of flame oil. As dawn broke the company returned to the starting position. The company reported two Flammpanzer as damaged beyond repair. One had been hit by gun fire from an enemy tank and the other had received a direct hit by an artillery shell. One sergeant and one man were wounded. One sergeant was missing.'

Employed on the Eastern Front, Panzer-Regiment 36 submitted the following experience report on 31 January 1944 dealing with the employment of their Panzer-Flamm-Zug: 'The Panzer-Flamm-Zug of the Regiment had only been in action twice. This mainly involved smoking out enemy positions. However, the desired results were not achieved. In spite of support from normal gun armed tanks, the large number of anti-tank rifles employed by the Russians and

*The business end of a Panzerkampfwagen III (Fl), tactical number 'F24'. The vehicle chassis number (Fahrgestell Nr. 77651) is painted on the front armour plate. Note the additional armour welded to the nose plates. The bar for carrying spare track links on the nose is missing. (US Official)*

the type of terrain in the southern sector of the Eastern Front (broad terrain without cover) caused Flammpanzer losses. During the first action, two Flammpanzer were destroyed by anti-tank guns and rifles. While flamethrowing, the Flammpanzer is visible from far away. It automatically draws long range enemy fire. The relatively thin armour, especially the vulnerable flamethrower tube, does not permit the Flammpanzer to concentrate on its assigned tasks without distractions.

'Therefore, the Flammpanzer can only succeed when employed in terrain with adequate cover (middle and north sectors of the Eastern Front). And then only if it is possible to neutralise defensive weapons within the range of the flamethrower in advance. This would naturally require that the armour protection be doubled and Schürzen (armour skirts) added for protection.

'In recognition of the few possibilities for employment (especially in the southern sector of the Eastern Front), the Regiment is using the remaining Flammpanzer mainly for guarding towns, employed beside normal gun-armed tanks. No specific technical breakdowns have occurred up to now.'

This report was forwarded to General Guderian (Generalinspekteur der Panzertruppen) through the headquarters of the 14 Panzer-Division and the XXXXVII Panzer-Korps, who added the following comments: 'The Panzer-Flamm-Zug could not be effectively used. The Flammpanzer can't be employed with the rest of the Panzer-Regiment. The necessary depth in the attacking tank formation can't be achieved in the current circumstances. Only 12 to 20 tanks are operational daily and infantry are not available in adequate numbers.'

During further operations in 1944, the number of operational Flammpanzer dwindled down to only six reported by the 26.Panzer-Division on 1 June 1944. Four Flammpanzer returned to the ordnance depot for major repairs had their chassis used for conversion to Sturmgeschuetz. In response to Hitler's order on 27 November 1944, that a large number of Flammpanzer (at least 20 to 30) were to be completed for a special action, at least ten Pz.Kpfw.III (Fl) were refurbished. Ten of these Panzerflammwagen III were issued to the newly created Panzer-Flamm-Kompanie 351.

A notice sent on 6 January 1945 by Generalmajor Guderian, informed Heeres Gruppe Sued that Panzer-Flamm-Kompanie 351 was to be held ready for action in Budapest. He also instructed that the company was to be attached to a Panzer-Regiment or Panzer-Abteilung. Still in action with Heeres Gruppe Sued on 10 April 1945, Flamm-Panzer-Kompanie 351 reported that they had four operational Pz.Kpfw.III (Fl) plus one in need of repair.

# STUG-I (FLAMM)

In a conference with Hitler on 1-3 December 1943, it was decided to outfit a single series of ten

*The commander of the Panzerkampfwagen III (Fl) was also the operator for the flame projector and turret MG. The two other crew members were the driver and the radio operator/hull machine gunner. (US Official)*

1: Panzerkampfwagen II (F) (Sd.Kfz.122)
Ausf.B, Russia, December 1941

2: Panzerkampfwagen B2 (F), Panzer Abteilung (F) 102,
Russia 1941

A

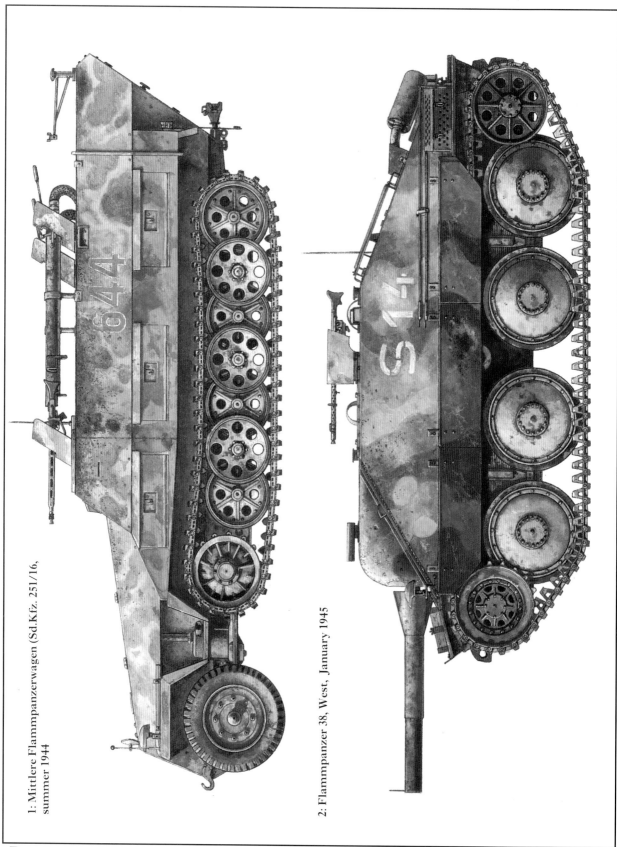

1: Mittlere Flammpanzerwagen (Sd.Kfz. 251/16, summer 1944

2: Flammpanzer 38, West, January 1945

B

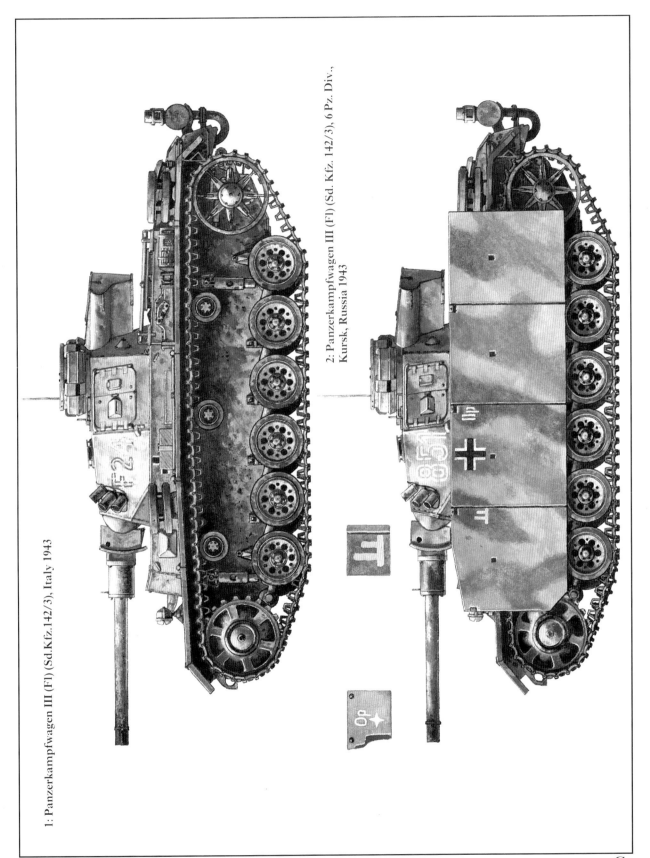

1: Panzerkampfwagen III (Fl) (Sd.Kfz.142/3), Italy 1943

2: Panzerkampfwagen III (Fl) (Sd. Kfz. 142/3), 6 Pz. Div., Kursk, Russia 1943

# PANZERKAMPFWAGEN III (FL)
## Panzerkampfwagen III (Fl) (Sd. Kfz. 142/3), Italy 1943

## SPECIFICATIONS

**Length:** 6.41 m
**Width:** 2.97 m
**Height:** 2.50 m
**Ground clearance:** .38 m
**Combat weight loaded:** 23.8 ton
**Fuel capacity:** 310 litres
**Maximum speed:** 40 km/h
**Cruising speed on roads:** 5 km/h
**Cross-country speed:** 15 km/h
**Range on roads:** 155 km
**Range cross-country:** 95 km
**Grade climbing ability:** 30 degrees
**Step climbing ability:** .60 m
**Trench crossing ability:** 2.00 m
**Fording depth:** .80 m
**Ground pressure:** 1.04 kg/cm²
**Power/weight ratio:** 11.5 metric HP/ton

## KEY

1. Steering brakes
2. Extra 30mm armour welded to 50mm nose plate
3. Extra 30mm armour welded to upper hull 50mm armour
4. Spare track links
5. SSG 77 transmission
6. Steering unit
7. Cooling air intakes
8. Hingeless access hatch
9. Spare track link rack
10. Machine gun ball mount
11. 20mm spaced armour plate
12. 50mm driver front plate
13. Radio rack
14. Flame thrower
15. Sighting vane for the commander
16. 20mm spaced armour in front of mantel
17. Smoke candle launchers
18. Elevation gear segment
19. Mounting for spring counter balance on gun tanks
20. Mantel/ Flame thrower counterweight
21. Flame oil pipe
22. Armoured cover over extractor fan
23. Flame oil pressure gauge
24. Flame thrower elevation hand wheel
25. Right hand side flame oil tank
26. Commanders cupola
27. Armoured visors on commander's cupola
28. Firewall between engine and fighting compartments
29. Pistol port in rear turret
30. Stowage bin
31. Maybach HL 120 main engine in motor compartment
32. Exhaust muffler with non return valve for submerging
33. Air intakes with submerging seal covers
34. Fire extinguisher
35. Jack
36. Shaft from turret ring to azimuth indicator
37. Gas mask container
38. Commander's seat
39. Toolbox
40. Crowbar
41. Auxiliary motor and pump for flame oil (in motor compartment)
42. Left hand side flame oil tank
43. Commanders' foot rests
44. Co-axial machine gun foot pedal trigger
45. Flame thrower foot pedal
46. Spare glass visor blocks
47. Turret traverse hand wheel
48. Turret fire extinguisher
49. Steering levels
50. Gear change lever
51. Headlight with black out cover

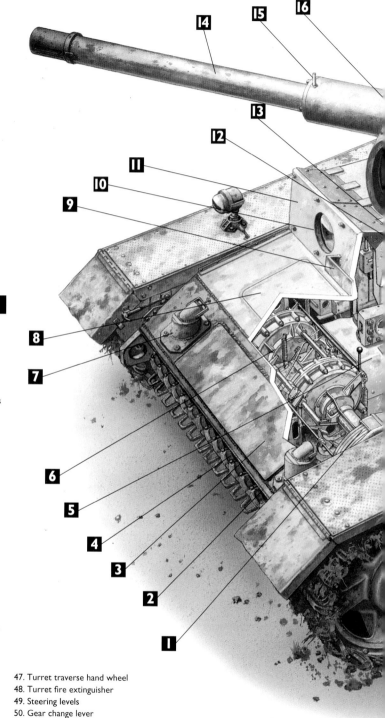

D

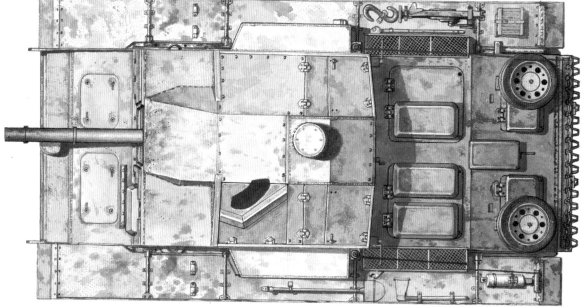

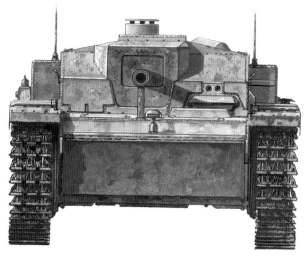

Sturmgeschutz (Flamm),
Panzertruppenschule I,
Germany 1943

E

1: Panzerkampfwagen II (F) (Sd. Kfz. 122)
Panzer Abteilung (F) 100, Russia 1941

F

Panzerkampfwagen B2 (F), 7 SS Freiwilligen Gebrigs Div. *'Prinz Eugen'*, Yugoslavia, May 1943

G

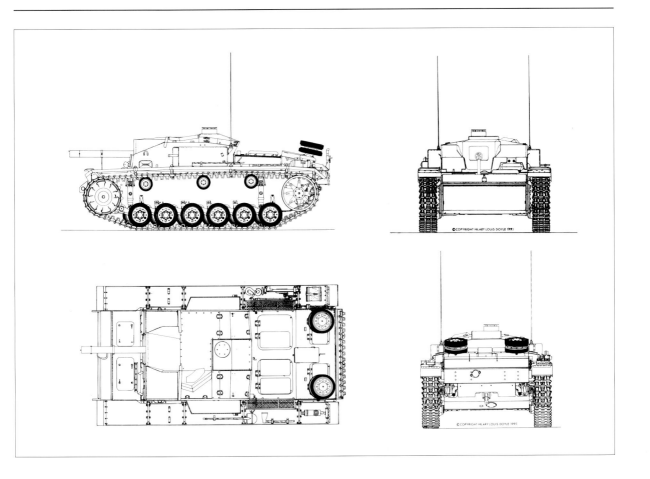

*A 1:76 scale drawing of the Sturmgeschütz (Flamm) III. (Author)*

Sturmgeschütz with flamethrowers. The Flammen-Anlage System Schwade (flamethrower system designed by Schwade) was to be installed. Initially the intention was to convert ten new Sturmgeschütz from the current production series. Instead of using newly produced chassis, the ten Sturmgeschütz (Flamm) were assembled utilising rebuilt chassis from older Sturmgeschütz that had been returned to the ordnance depot for major repair and overhaul. Original Waffenamt reports record that nine Sturmgeschütz (Flamm) were delivered to the ordnance depot 'aus Instandsetzung' (from major rebuild) in May 1943 and the final one Sturmgeschütz (Flamm) was delivered in June 1943.

These ten Sturmgeschütz (Flamm) were issued to Panzertruppenschule I and were shipped by rail to this unit on 29 June 1943. A note on the issue records stated that one of the ten Sturmgeschütz (Flamm) had caught fire and burnt out. This Sturmgeschütz (Flamm) was sent back in July

1943, repaired, and returned to the unit in September 1943. Records have not been found revealing that any of these ten Sturmgeschütz (Flamm) were used in combat. All ten were returned to the ordnance depot in January 1944. Seven in February, one in March, and two in April 1944 were converted back to normal Sturmgeschütz mounting the 7.5 cm Sturmkanone 40 L/48.

# SD.KFZ.251/16

## Description and Specifications

A flamethrower system similar to the one developed for the Pz.Kpfw.B2 (Fl) was mounted in a mittlere Schützen-Panzer-Wagen (Sd.Kfz.251)

(medium armoured personnel carrier). This Flammanlage Bauart Koebe (Koebe design flamethrower system) consisted of one DKW-Motor driving a Koebe pump; two 14 mm Strahlrohren (spray tubes) with quick closing valves and closer caps, each with an armour shield; one 7 mm Strahlrohr with a 10 m long hose and a second 10 m extension hose; and two flame oil containers with associated pipes and valves. The complete assembly added 850 kg to the weight of the vehicle.

A 14 mm Strahlrohr with its armour shield was mounted toward the rear on both the right and left side of the vehicle. Each of these side mounted flamethrowers could be traversed through an arc of 160°. The hand-held 7 mm

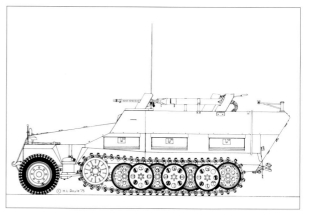

*A 1:76 scale drawing of the Flamm-panzerwagen Sd. Kfz. 251/16 left hand side view. (Author)*

### Table 6: m.Flamm.Pz.Wg Specifications

Length: *5.80 m*
Width: *2.10 m*
Height: *2.10 m*
Ground clearance: *0.32 m*
Weight (combat loaded): *8.62 t*
Fuel capacity: *160 litres*
Max. speed: *50 km/h*
Range (on roads): *300 km*
Range (cross-country): *150 km*
Max. gradient: *24°*
Trench crossing ability: *2.00 m*
Fording depth: *0.50 m*
Power-to-weight ratio: *11.6 metric hp/ton*

Strahlrohr with flexible hose was stored in a coiled position at the rear of the vehicle.

Two containers (one mounted inside the left rear side wall and one mounted inside the right rear side wall) held a total of 700 litres of Flammöl Nr.19 flame oil. This was sufficient fuel for approximately 80 one second spurts. Eight litres of flame oil were discharged per second of operation of the main side mounted flamethrowers.

When fired separately, each of the side mounted flame throwers with 14 mm nozzles could achieve a range of 50 m with cold flame oil (60 m when ignited). When fired together, the resultant pressure drop shortened the range. With closed valves a pressure of 15 atmospheres was

*Two 14 mm projectors were mounted one on either side of the Sd.Kfz.251/16 and a 7 mm projector with a hose extension was stored at the rear. (Author)*

built up by the Koebe pump. When spraying with one 14 mm nozzle, the pressure decreased to 13 atmospheres at a delivered flow rate of 8 lit/sec. The Koebe HL II 40/40 1000/200 pump was driven by a two-stroke, 28 metric hp, 1100 cc, Auto-Union ZW 1101 (DKW) engine running off a mixture of oil and petrol. The 25 litre fuel supply for the DKW engine was sufficient for two hours of operation at full power.

The flame oil sprayed from the 14 mm nozzles was ignited by electrical Spezial-Zündkerzen (special ignition plugs). The flame oil sprayed from the hand-held 7 mm nozzle was ignited by Mauser-Patronen (cartridges).

As revealed in the user manual D 546/4, several modifications were made to the flamethrower system by May 1944. The two side mounted 14 mm spray nozzles were redesigned. In the new system Patronen (blank cartridges) for ignition of the flame oil replaced the previous Benzin-electric ignition system. A magazine containing 25 blank cartridges was inserted into this new Patronenstrahlrohr. In addition, the armoured shields were redesigned and the hand-held 7 mm nozzle was deleted. An MG34 was mounted at the front of the crew compartment in a swivel mount with an armoured shield. The crew also possessed two MP38 machine pistols. Magazines containing 2,010 rounds for the MG and 1,024 rounds for

*The auxiliary motor and fuel pump before being mounted in an early version of the Sd.Kfz.251/16. This photo was taken at the Koebe factory. (Author)*

the machine pistols were the authorised ammunition load for this vehicle.

A crew of four manned this 8.62 ton Flammpanzerwagen. The Flammführer (commander) also served as the Funksprechgerät 'f' radio operator and manned the MG. Two Flammschützen (flamethrower operators) were assigned, one for each flamethrower. The Fahrer (driver) was located in the left front.

Armour protection for the chassis consisted of 14.5 mm thick plates on the front and 8 mm thick plates for the sides and rear. The layout of the armour plates was adequate to provide protection against armour-piercing rounds fired from small arms (8 mm and less) at all ranges.

The HKL6p chassis was designed by Hanomag, Hannover. Power was provided by a six-cylinder, water-cooled, 4.198 litre, Maybach HL 42 TUKRM petrol engine delivering 100 hp (metric) at 3,000 rpm. A four-speed transmission with a high/low ratio transfer case transferred the power through the planetary gears and steering brake unit and final drives to the drive sprockets propelling the tracks. Each of the six road wheels

*Rear view of the Sd.Kfz.251/16, which was based on the Ausf.C version of the m.SPW. The open rear doors reveal the pump and auxiliary motor. (Tank Museum)*

*Detail of the flame projector on the right-hand side of a Sd.Kfz.251/16. The fuel for the flamethrower is stored in the tank beneath the projector. (Tank Museum)*

mounted on each side were sprung by independent torsion bar suspension.

## Production

Production of the mittlere Flammpanzerwagen was first recorded by the Waffenamt in reports for January 1943.

After reporting a total of 96 completed in the period from January through July 1943, the Waffenamt ceased recording the number produced. This was not unusual. For most of the production period from 1939 through 1945, the Waffenamt did not bother to report the number of each variant of the Sd.Kfz.251 that left the production line each month.

A planning document dated 1 October 1944, stated that the Sd.Kfz.251/16 was being assembled by Wumag, Görlitz and revealed the production plans for the period from October 1944 through May 1945. Starting with September 1944, in addition to reporting the total number of Sd.Kfz.251 produced each month, the Waffenamt reported the number of several variants accepted for issue. A total of 293 Sd.Kfz.251/16 were reported in the inventory on 1 September 1944. This reveals that at least 200 fuly operational

*Sd.Kfz.251/16 based on the m.SPW Ausf.D. By May 1944 the spray nozzles and shields had been redesigned. Ignition was achieved by firing blank cartridges. The hand-held projector had to be deleted. (Bundesarchiv)*

Sd.Kfz.251/16 had been produced between August 1943 and August 1944.

## Organisation and Combat Reports

Initially in 1943, six Sd.Kfz.251/16 were issued to a Flamm-Zug (flamethrower platoon) attached to the Stabskompanie of the Panzer-Grenadier-Regiments a (gp). The Flamm-Zug (gp) organised in accordance with K.St.N.1130 dated 1 August 1943 was listed as a Teil-Einheit (partial unit). This organisational structure was changed when the unit was incorporated as the 2. (Flamm) Zug with six mittlere Flammpanzerwagen (Sd.Kfz.251/16) as an integral part of the Stab und Stabskompanie/Panzer-Grenadier-Regiments a (gp) in accordance with K.St.N.1104 a gp dated 1 November 1943.

By early 1944, the Flamm-Zug was removed from the Stabskompanie. In accordance with K. St.N.1118 Ausf.B dated 1 April and 1 November 1944, the six mittlere Flammpanzerwagen (Sd.Kfz.251/16) were in the 4. (Flamm) Zug (gp.)

*Close up of the later projector and shield on a Sd.Kfz.251/16. (Bundesarchiv)*

of the Panzergrenadier-Pionier-Kompanie in the Panzer-Grenadier-Regiments (gp). From start to finish, only six Sd.Kfz.251/16 were authorised in the organisation of each Panzer-Grenadier-Regiment (gp). Therefore, with rare exceptions such as the Panzer-Lehr Division with two Panzer-Grenadier-Regiments (gp), only six Sd.Kfz.251/16 were authorised for each Panzer-Division.

Publication of a new K.St.N. did not entitle a unit to automatically change its organisation or result in the issue of new vehicles to it. Specific orders, created by the Organisations-Abteilung of the Oberkommando des Heeres, authorised changes to organisations. The vehicles themselves were issued from the ordnance depots by another set of orders from Chef Heeres Rustung. Starting in 1943, orders were cut to form new Flamm-Züge as additional Sd.Kfz.251/16 became available. But this was a slow process. By mid 1944, only about half of the Panzer-Divisions possessed a Flamm-Zug with Sd.Kfz.251/16. The independent Panzer-Brigaden, formed from July to September 1944, were also authorised to have a Panzergrenadier-Pionier-Kompanie with a Flamm-

Zug with six Sd.Kfz.251/16.

On 1 February 1944, Panzer-Grenadier-Division 'Grossdeutschland' reported their experiences with the mittlere Flammpanzerwagen (Sd.Kfz.251/16). Since 27 June 1943, the Stabs-Kompanie of Panzer-Grenadier Regiment 'Grossdeutschland' had possessed a Flamm-Zug with a strength of six mittlere Flammpanzerwagen. The following experience was gained duing 14 separate actions.

A. Tactical: 'The mittlere Flammpanzerwagen has proven to be a highly valued weapon when correctly employed in the hands of an energetic and observant platoon leader. The successes are expected to increase with increased familiarity and experience of the crews.

'During employment within a tank attack, special attention must be paid to eliminating enemy tanks and anti-tank guns, whose hits will immediately knock the Flammpanzer out of action. For this type of action, the same basic tactical principles apply that govern the employment of other Sd.Kfz.251.

'Employment in tank attacks is not the intended role of the Flammpanzerwagen. In general, the Flamm-Zug should remain as the last reserve in the hands of the regimental commander. The best results have then been achieved through swift and smart attacks conducted without the aid of supporting weapons.

'Surprise attacks against enemy groups that have broken into our positions, fully utilising the flamethrower power of all Flammpanzerwagen, have proven to be very effective. This is especially true for rapid counter-attacks when the enemy anti-tank guns and rifles are still not in position and aren't familiar with the surrounding terrain. In an action lasting 45 minutes, a reckless charge resulted in unique success. Eighty enemy died as a result of burns, 20 were wounded, and about 20 prisoners were brought in. The rest of the enemy group threw away their weapons and fled.

'The employment of the Flammpanzerwagen is especially effective at night. In spite of revealing their positions on the nighttime battlefield by their spurts of flame, very seldom were Flammpanzerwagen knocked out of action by hits from anti-tank guns. The intense glare from the flames contributes to substantial estimation and range errors by the crews of the enemy anti-tank guns.

'The flamethrowers have a very large demoralising effect at night. An additional advantage is that the battlefield is illuminated for own attacking forces. Several night attacks have resulted in substantial successes, completely eliminating weaker enemy battle groups. The Flammpanzerwagen has also proven to be effective in combat in maize and sunflower fields.

'An additional, as high as possible, supply of hand grenades and machine pistol ammunition is necessary. The basic tactical rule must always be swift and surprising attacks by the Flamm-Zug. A reckless charge, fully employing the flamethrowers, hand grenades and machine pistol, must follow after a quick scouting patrol. There can never be enough consideration applied to the selection of the leader of the Flamm-Zug.'

B. Technical: 'It is completely unnecessary to outfit the Flammpanzerwagen with the hand-held flamethrower on the rear. The large area traversed by both of the main flamethrowers, that can be further enlarged by turning the vehicle, is sufficient for engaging any bunker openings, cellar entrances, or individual hidden fox holes. If one of the main flamethrowers becomes unserviceable during the battle, it takes too long to bring the hand-held flamethrower into action. The freed crew member should immediately attack with hand grenades or machine pistol, utilising every costly minute to destroy the opponent that the Flammpanzerwagen is overrunning.

'A large number of hits from small arms fire, deflected off the armour shield for the machine gun, have incapacitated the crew manning the flamethrowers. Widening the armour shield by 20 cm would decrease injuries to crew members.

'A second receiving radio set is necessary for the platoon leader to communicate with supporting Panzer or Sturmgeschütz.

'It is proposed that a howling siren be installed to add to the demoralising effect of the flamethrowers. The siren can be driven by the pump motor.

As a result of inadequate ventilation, the main motor overheats during marches in the summer. Opening the hatches over the motor compartment does not eliminate overheating. It is proposed that an opening again be installed in the frontal armour that can be shut during action.'

# FLAMMPANZER 38

On 27 November 1944, Hitler ordered that in a special action a large number of Flammpanzer (at

*The crew of this Sd.Kfz.251/16 are wearing the special protective clothing issued to flamethrower troops. This vehicle was issued to a unit of the 1.SS Panzer Division Leibstandarte 'Adolf Hitler' (Bundesarchiv)*

least 20-30) were to be completed. The next day, Hitler ordered an immediate determination of how many Flammenwerferwagen could be completed from available Panzer or Sturmgeschütz chassis in the next three days. On 3 December, Hitler received a report that the ordered Flammenwerfer action was on schedule with an expected total of 35 Flammpanzer. Along with refurbishing at least ten Pz.Kpfw.III (Fl), twenty Jagdpanzer 38 were selected for conversion to Flammpanzer 38.

Twenty Jagdpanzer 38 were obtained directly from the factory for conversion to Flammpanzer on 8 December 1944. A Flammpanzer 38 captured by American forces had Fgst.Nr. 322091, proving that its chassis was completed in December 1944. On 3 January 1945, Hitler was shown photographs of the single series of Flammpanzer 38 and Flammpanzer III.

### Description and Specifications

The Koebe Flammenwerfer was mounted in the hull front in a swivel mount allowing only limited traverse and elevation. A container with 700 litres of flame oil was considered sufficient for 60 to 70 bursts. The propelling force was provided by pressure from a pump. The flame oil was ignited using cartridges. An MG34 on the roof had a unique mount with a periscope that allowed the MG to be fired while buttoned up. A crew of four manned this 13.5 ton Flammpanzer.

The armour protection consisted of 60 mm plates on the front and 20 mm plates for the sides and rear. The well-sloped front plates provided adequate protection against any hits from tank or anti-tank guns from the front. The sides were only designed to withstand hits from armour piercing rounds fired from small arms or hits from artillery shell splinters.

The chassis was that of a normal Jagdpanzer 38. Power was provided by a six-cylinder, water-cooled, 7.754 litre, Praga AC petrol engine delivering 160 bhp (metric) at 2600 rpm.

A semi-automatic five-speed transmission transferred power forward through the Wilson clutch and brake steering unit and final drives to the drive sprockets propelling the tracks. The four large diameter road wheels mounted on each side were sprung in pairs by leaf springs.

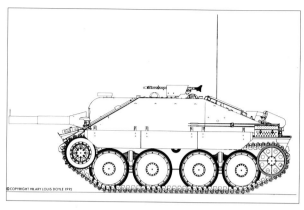

*A 1:76 scale drawing of the Flamm-Panzer 38 left hand side view. (Author)*

## Table 7: Flammpanzer 38 Specifications

Length: *4.87 m*
Width: *2.63 m*
Height: *2.10 m*
Ground clearance: *0.38 m*
Weight (combat loaded): *13.5 t*
Fuel capacity: *320 litres*
Max. speed: *40 km/h*
Cruising speed *(on roads)*: *30 km/h*
Cross-country speed: *15 km/h*
Range (on roads): *180 km*
Range (cross-country): *130 km*
Max. gradient: *25°*
Step climbing ability: *0.65 m*
Trench crossing ability: *1.30 m*
Fording depth: *0.90 m*
Ground pressure: *0.78 kg/cm2*
Power-to-weight ratio: *11.8 metric hp/ton*

### Organisation and Experience Report

On 26 December 1944, Heeres Gruppe G reported that two Flamm-Panzer-Kompanien each with ten Flammpanzer were being transported to Zweibrücken. Panzer-Flamm-Kompanie 352 had started forward on 25 December and Panzer-Flamm-Kompanie 353 was to start forward on 30 December 1944. The planned initial action for both Flamm-Panzer-Kompanien was to be in the leading attack group in Unternehmen 'Nordwind' (Operation 'Northwind') and not in the Ardennes offensive as has been falsely reported.

On 31 December 1944, Heeres Gruppe G provided Armee Oberkommando 1 with the following instructions for the employment of Panzer-

*The flame tube is intact on this Flammpanzer 38. A periscope is mounted in the top of the ball mantle. (US Official)*

Flamm-Kompanie 352 and 353:

1. Panzer-Flamm-Kompanie 352 und 353 are each outfitted with 10 Panzer-Flamm-Wagen 38(t) mit Koebe-Gerät. The range of the flamethrowers is 35 m.
2. They are only to be employed concentrated, considering the potential for utilisation of the weapon's technical capabilities.
3. Tactical principles are contained in pamphlets numbered 75/1 and 75/2.
4. Without exception, Panzer-Flamm-Kompanien are to be attached to Panzer-Regiments or Panzer-Abteilungen.
5. Isolated employment is forbidden.

Panzer-Flamm-Kompanie 352 submitted the following experience report on the employment of Flammpanzer 38 dated 23 February 1945:

Panzer-Flamm-Kompanie 352 attached to Panzer-Abteilung 5 (25. Panzer-Grenadier-Division) was first employed in combat in an attack on Hatten. Having already lost all of its officers and seven Flamm-Panzer 38, the remainder of Panzer-Flamm-Kompanie 353 was absorbed into the 352nd. During this action the Flammpanzer were mainly used against bunkers and field works. In addition, the Flammpanzer assaulted the village of Hatten without escorting infantry or accompanying tanks.

A second action occurred in street fighting in Rittershofen, whereby two Flammpanzer were destroyed by an enemy anti-tank gun and a tank. A further Flammpanzer drove over a mine and after recovering the weapons had to be abandoned. Subsequently, due to additional hits from enemy fire, this Flammpanzer was damaged beyond repair. These actions revealed the following:

1. The Jagdpanzer 38 is a mature automotive design, capable of negotiating the terrain. Through its low profile and speed, they are manoeuvrable and can quickly be driven into cover. Replacing the main gun with the flamethrower eliminated the front heaviness, which improved the function of the steering gears. The power-to-weight ratio (160 metric horse-power for 13.5 metric tons) is very useful.

2. The frontal armour is sufficient and safe from attack. A round fired by an enemy 76.2 mm anti-tank gun from a close range failed to penetrate the frontal armour. The side armor is weak but safe from attack of anti-tank rifles and artillery shell splinters. A weld seam failed as a result of a hit on the front plates of one Flammpanzer.

3. The built-in flamethrower and flame oil tanks functioned perfectly without failures. The

*Side view of a Flamm-panzer 38 captured by the Americans. These Flamm-panzer were converted from 20 Jagdpanzer 38 built by BMM in Prague in 1944. The flame projector system is identical to that developed for the Sd.Kfz.251/16 with cartridge ignition. (US Official)*

tube covering intended to camouflage the flamethrower is much too weak. It is very easily bent and immediately penetrated by small arms fire. This causes malfunctions in the flamethrower that would not occur if the cover was left off altogether.

The range of 50 m is insufficient. It is desired that the range be doubled. Targets could then be engaged that can't be closely approached (bunkers behind wire entanglements, obstacles protected by mines, etc.). The flamethrower device itself must be better protected with a cover against dampness and damage by crew members entering and leaving the Flammpanzer. The gaskets must be improved. After some time, the flame oil leaks, if only in small amounts, creating a fire hazard – especially in the motor. The main hose to the flamethrower must be mounted a bit further to the right. It hinders free movement by the gunner.

4. The additional weapons and MG34 mount have turned out to be correct and necessary. Drum or belt fed ammunition is equally acceptable.

5. Experience has proven that the decision, made during creation of the organisation to increase the crew to four men (driver, flamethrower operator, radio operator, and commander), was correct. In comparison, the original plans were for a crew of three (driver, flamethrower operator, and commander also dou-

bling as radio operator). Also, the hatch added for the radio operator was correct, allowing complete access to the machine gun. Other then this, an escape hatch is needed and would be useful.

6. The flame oil tanks in each Flammpanzer contain 700 litres, so that one fill is sufficient for 60-70 spurts. The flamethrowers can discharge either a cold spry or a burning spray after it is ignited with Zuendpatrone (ignition cartridges). Field emplacements (trenches, fox holes, etc.) should first be covered with a cold spray, so that the flame oil sinks into the holes. This is followed by a burning spray to ignite the initial cold spray. A delayed reaction is achieved that is useful for engaging trenches that can't always be successfully engaged with a pre-ignited spray. The same method applies to engaging bunkers (other than wooden bunkers that are directly burnt) and basements. All other targets are engaged with pre-ignited spray.

The effect of the flame oil is both corrosive and burning. If personnel that are hit are not completely incinerated, they receive very severe burns. The flame oil itself has a very painful corrosive effect and creates intense heat when burning. When hit, flammable parts of weapons and equipment immediately burn; other parts are rendered unusable. Houses, especially frame houses and wooden houses, are immediately ignited by the relatively long burning oil. The ability to resist in attacked bunkers is greatly hindered by the heat and the resulting strong and biting smoke. Their ability to fight is very strongly eroded, if not fully suppressed.

Success against tanks can only be achieved by a surprise attack from close range, since the Flammpanzer itself does not possess a heavy weapon. The only possibilities that remain are to try to set the motor of the tank on fire or to interfere with their vision by engaging the enemy tank with ignited spurts.

The spurts of flame with associated large clouds of smoke have a demoralising effect on the opponent that is not to be underestimated. The action against and in Hatten on 9 January 1945, has shown that the Western opponent is very susceptible to the actual and demoralising effects of the Flammpanzer.

7. Basically, the Flammpanzer can only be employed in association with tanks or swift, manoeuvrable anti-tank weapons. As a result of the lack of anti-tank weapons, the Flammpanzer itself is defenceless against enemy tanks and anti-tank guns. As a consequence of its weapons and armour, the Flammpanzer is very good in providing effective support when attacking infantry in bunkers and field fortifications and in combat in towns and in the forest. During combat in towns or in the forest, the Flammpanzer must be accompanied by infantry to protect it during close-combat and to occupy the smoked out areas. In defence, the Flammpanzer should be used in counter-attacks, again accompanied by tanks. Single Flammpanzer should never be employed alone. They should be used in at least platoon sized units and for best results as the entire company.

Flamm-Panzer-Kompanie 352 reported that they still had 11 Flamm-Panzer 38 of which eight were operational on 15 March 1945.

# TIGER I

In a conference on 5 December 1944, Hitler suggested that in order to achieve its role, a lead vehicle needed a long range flamethrower

*Front view of the Flammpanzer 38 captured by American forces. The protective tube over the flame projector is damaged, a weakness detailed in the experience report in the main text. (US Official)*

mounted behind the heaviest armour possible. This should be a heavy tank, easily the Tiger. At a conference on 29 December 1944, Hitler again stated that only tanks with the heaviest armour and flamethrowers with a long range could be used as a Flammpanzer. He also considered using the Jagdtiger if a range of 200 m could be achieved. At the conference on 3 January 1945, Hitler again emphasised the importance of developing a heavy Flammpanzer with 250 mm thick armour.

In a meeting of the Entwicklungskommission Panzer on 23. January 1945, Oberst Crohn reported on the status of the development of the Flammpanzer. By using compressed nitrogen, a range of 120-140 m was achievable with the newly developed large flamethrower. The pressure in the flame oil tanks must be at 20-25 atmospheres to achieve this range. It was possible to install the flamethrower nozzle in a Tiger in a fixed position where the hull MG was mounted. 800 litres of flame oil (2 x 400 litre tanks) could be carried inside the Tiger. This would be sufficient flame oil for 16-20 spurts. With internal flame oil stowage, additional weapons systems couldn't be mounted in the Tiger.

Another suggested solution was to use a trailer to haul the flame oil. It would then be possible to retain the Tiger's weapon systems.

Oberstlt. Otto added that they had recently created a mount for the 120-140 m range flamethrower nozzle that was traversable 10° in all directions. A fluid pump could not used because the flame oil had been thickened to achieve the longer range. The thicker flame oil must be propelled by nitrogen pressurised in compressed gas cylinders or the pressure increased by using reduction valves. Special reduction valves with a 10 mm cross section were necessary and could be obtained from the German navy.

General-Major Thomale imparted that the troops had previously rejected the Flammpanzer. But the troops had again requested a Flammpanzer after it was employed by the enemy. Considering the known advantages and disadvantages of the Flammpanzer, he liked flamethrowers mounted in small armored vehicles that could pick off fox holes and nests of resistance with their tra-

versable flamethrowers. He emphasised that the Tiger I could successfully engage the enemy at a combat range of 2500 m with its 8,8 cm Kw.K. L/56 and 80 rounds of ammunition. A Tiger as a Flammpanzer can only discharge 16-20 spurts at a range of 120-140 m. From a soldier's standpoint, conversion of a Tiger I into a Flammtiger was in no way acceptable.

Further experiments and tests still needed to be conducted on the new flamethrower device. A further consideration was that Tiger production had appreciably reduced due to bombing raids. Dr. von Heydekampf recognised these military and technical positions but declared that since this idea was a directive from Hitler, further development of the Flammpanzer must be pursued.

The general consensus of the committee was that the Tiger was to valuable to be a carrier for a flamethrower. But a flamethrower mounted in a Jagdpanzer 38 would be acceptable.

On 19 March 1945, the Flammanlage auf Tiger I was included in a report on active development projects that were to be continued in spite of the deteriorating situation. Hitler in a meeting with Generalleutnant Thomale again specifically ordered that a experimental copy of a flamethrower with a range of 100-120 m was to be mounted on a turretless Tiger chassis and quickly completed. Hitler wanted chemists to direct their energy into making German flame oil with the same characteristics as the British flame oil. He also suggested strengthening the frontal armour to compensate for the short flamethrower range of 100-120 m. On 3 April 1945, Oberst Holzhäuer, head of Wa Prüf 6, reported the progress achieved in meeting Hitler's demand for a Schwerst-Flammpanzer auf Tiger I (heaviest flamethrower tank on a Tiger I chassis). The first meeting on fabricating this experimental Flammpanzer had occurred at Wegmann, Kassel on 21/22 March 1945. Wegmann had agreed to complete the Flammpanzer by 15 April under the condition that the Tiger I to be converted and the Stickstoffflammgeräts (compressed nitrogen, flame thrower assembly) to be installed were delivered on schedule.

Both the Tiger I and the experimental Stickstoffflammgerät had been loaded on a train with the highest priority orders and left Kummersdorf bound for Kassel on 17 March 1945. In spite of continuous harassment of the transport commander in Berlin, the railcar had still not arrived in Kassel as of 3 April 1945. As a result of the confused situation in Kassel, Wegmann was advised that the railcar should be diverted to Miag in Braunschweig. The prototype of the Flammpanzer was then to be assembled under the direction of Wegmann personnel at the Miag facilities in Braunschweig.

Due to the loss of 17 days in transport, the completion of an operational, experimental Flammpanzer was no longer expected to occur by 15 April 1945. Further Allied troop advances and the bombing campaign disrupted any further activity associated with the completion of this experimental Schwerst-Flammpanzer auf Tiger I.

*The second series of the Panzerkampfwagen B2 (F) had a new flame projector system. The projector was again mounted in place of the 75 mm hull gun of the original French Char B, but the pressure for the flame fuel was provided by an auxiliary motor. First deliveries of these conversions began in November-December 1941. (Werner Regenberg)*

# THE PLATES

**Plate A1:** *Panzerkampfwagen II (F) (Sd.K fz. 122) Ausf.B, Russia, December 1941*
After the first series of 90 Panzerkampfwagen II (F) had been produced a further 150 additional Panzerkampfwagen II (F) were ordered. In August 1941, production of these 2. Serie La.S.138 (2nd Series) had already commenced.

In December 1941 it was decided to use these chassis for mounting the 7.62 cm Pak 36 (r) instead of Flammpanzer. Only 62 of the Panzerkampfwagen II (F) Ausf.B had been completed when production stopped in March 1942. All tanks completed in 1941 were painted in dunkelgrau RAL 7021 (Dark grey)

**Plate A2:** *Panzerkampfwagen B2 (F), Panzer Abteilung (F) 102, Russia 1941*
After the decision to mount anti-tank guns on the chassis ordered for the Panzerkampfwagen II (F) Ausf.B, a new plan was made to continue producing Flammpanzer. This called for the conversion of captured French Char B1*bis* heavy tanks. The Panzerkampfwagen B2, as the Char B1*bis* was called by the Germans, was more heavily armoured than the Panzerkampfwagen II. The

first series conversion was achieved by mounting one of the Flammenwerfer-SpritzKöpf (flamethrower spray head) from the Panzerkampfwagen II (F) in place of the hull mounted 7.5 cm of the Pz.Kpfw.B2. The 4.7 cm Kw.K. (f) was retained in the turret. German tanks of this period were painted in dunkelgrau RAL 7021 (Dark grey) and the Panzerkampfwagen B2 (F) were repainted in this colour during their refitting period.

**Plate B1:** *Mittlere Flammpanzerwagen (Sd Kfz 251/16), summer 1944*
Initially, the Sd.Kfz.251/16 were built on the Sd.Kfz.251 Ausf.C chassis. Our subject is based on the Sd.Kfz.251 Ausf.D. At this period German armour was painted with a base coat of dunkelgelb (Dark yellow) and if required it was oversprayed with irregular patches and stripes of olivgrün RAL 6003 (Dark olive green) and rotbraun RAL 8017 (Dark chocolate brown). The interior was also painted in dunkelgelb (Dark yellow)

**Plate B2:** *Flammpanzer 38, West, January 1945*
Two Flammpanzer Kompanie, the 352 and 353, were each equipped with ten Flammpanzer 38 converted from Jagdpanzer 38 taken from the pro-

*A flamethrower system similar to that developed for the Panzerkampfwagen B2 (F) was modified for mounting in the mittlerer Schützen-Panzer-Wagen Sd.Kfz.51 Ausf.C (medium armoured personnel carrier) from January 1943. This Flammpanzerwagen was designated Sd.Kfz.251/16. (Author)*

duction lines of BMM in Prague on the 8 December 1944. The plan was to use both Kompanie in Operation 'Nordwind'. The camouflage paint was applied at the Czech factory so as to save paint stocks. The basic rot RAL 8012 (Red primer) was overpainted by hand with irregular camouflage stripes of well-thinned olivgrün RAL 6003 (Dark olive green) and dunkelgelb (Dark yellow).

### Plate C1: *Panzerkampfwagen III (Fl) (Sd.Kfz.142/3), Italy 1943*

The Panzerkampfwagen III (Fl) was converted from 100 Panzerkampfwagen III Ausf.M chassis completed by Miag in Braunsweig. These were delivered to Wegmann in Kassel and completed as Panzerkampfwagen III (Fl). Additional flame fuel tanks, auxiliary motor, pump and associated projector pipework were installed. Wegmann mounted a modified Pz.Kpfw.III turret with the flamethrower in place of the 5 cm Kw.K. L/60. This is the same vehicle as shown in the cutaway – one of 21 Panzerkampfwagen III (Fl) which served in Italy. Seven were issued to the 16.Panzer Division and 14 to the 26.Panzer Division.

The exterior was painted in the dunkelgelb RAL 7028 (Tan), applied from February 1943. The crew were permitted to apply camouflage patterns of stripes and patches of olivgrün RAL 6003 (Dark olive green) and rotbraun RAL 8017

(Dark chocolate brown) over the base dunkelgelb. The Panzerkampfwagen III (Fl) of this unit were not camouflaged, but the tactical number on the turret has been changed.

### Plate C2: *Panzerkampfwagen III (Fl) (Sd.Kfz. 142/3), 6.Panzer Division, Kursk, Russia 1943*

This Panzerkampfwagen III (Fl), tactical number '851' of the 6.Panzer Division was retrofitted with Schürtzen (Apron armour) to protect the hull sides from the Russian anti-tank rifle fire. The Divisional sign, painted in yellow, on the Schürtzen is one of the so-called Kursk markings. In May 1943 the OKH Gruppe Süd issued a list of new divisional symbols which could be applied at short notice. The purpose of the symbols was to confuse the Russian intelligence. These markings were painted on most armoured vehicles just before Operation 'Zitadelle', the battle of Kursk. The letters 'Op' are thought to be the initials of the unit commander as they appear on other Panzerkampfwagen III Ausf.M and N of the unit.

### Plate D: *Panzerkampfwagen III (Fl) (Sd. Kfz. 142/3), Italy 1943*

The Panzerkampfwagen III (Fl) was converted from 100 Panzerkampfwagen III Ausf.M chassis that had been completed by Miag in Braunsweig. These were delivered to Wegmann in Kassel where they were completed as the Panzerkampfwagen III (Fl). The additional flame fuel tanks, auxiliary motor, pump and associated projector pipework were installed. Wegmann then mounted, a modified Panzerkampfwagen III turret with the flamethrower in place of the 5 cm Kw.K. L/60.

The cutaway shows a Panzerkampfwagen III (Fl) used in Italy and subsequently captured by the Allies. A total of 21 Panzerkampfwagen III (Fl) served in Italy. Seven were issued to the 16.Panzer Division and a further 14 to the 26.Panzer Division.

The exterior was painted in the dunkelgelb RAL 7028 (Tan), in use from February 1943. The crew were permitted to apply camouflage patterns of stripes and patches of olivgrün RAL 6003 (Dark olive green) and rotbraun RAL 8017 (Dark chocolate brown) over the base dunkelgelb. The

dunkelgelb RAL 7028 (Tan).

*The commander of the Panzerkampfwagen III (Fl) was also the operator for the flame projector and turret MG. The two other crew members were the driver and the radio operator/hull machine gunner. (US Official)*

Panzerkampfwagen III (Fl) of this unit were not camouflaged. The fighting compartment interior of all German armoured vehicles of this period were painted in elfenbein RAL 1002 (beige). Radio sets were dunkelgrau RAL 7021 (dark grey). The motor compartment was left in rot RAL 8012 (Red primer) while the Maybach HL 120 motor was grundierfarbe hellgrau RAL 7009 (Grey green undercoat).

## Plate E: *Sturmgeschütz (Fl), Panzer-truppen-schule I, Germany 1943*
Ten rebuilt Sturmgeschütz were converted to Sturmgeschütz (Flamm) in May and June 1943. They were issued to Panzertruppenschule I (Armoured Training School I ). In January 1944 they were returned to the Ordnance depot and over the coming months were reconverted to Sturmgeschütz mounting the 7.5 cm Sturmkanone 40 L/48.

This Sturmgeschütz (Flamm) was converted from a Sturmgeschütz Ausf.F/8 which was the first Sturmgeschütz to use the 8. Serie/Z.W. chassis introduced on the Pz.Kpfw.III Ausf.J. Additional armour was welded to the front surfaces, increasing their thickness to 80 mm. Armoured vehicles of this period were painted in

## Plate F: *Panzerkampfwagen II (F) (Sd. Kfz. 122) Panzer Abteilung (F) 100, Russia 1941*
A total of 46 1.Serie Panzerkampfwagen II (F) were built using new La.S.138 chassis. A few of these were the chassis designed for the Panzerkampfwagen II Ausf.E (Fahrgestell Nr. 27801-28000). The Ausf.E can be identified by the lubricated track, which was much deeper than the normal normal dry pin steel tracks used by the Ausf.D. An additional 43 Panzerkampfwagen II Ausf.D. (Fahrgestell Nr. 27001-27800) were returned by the troops for the conversion. Tanks delivered before August 1940 had the standard two colour camouflage of dunkelgrau RAL 7021 (Dark grey) and dunkelbraun RAL 7018 (Dark brown). From August 1940 all tanks were painted only in the dunkelgrau RAL 7021 (Dark grey).

## Plate G: *Panzerkampfwagen B2 (F), 7.SS Freiwilligen Gebrigs Division 'Prinz Eugen', Yugoslavia, May 1943*
This is one of the last production series of Panzerkampfwagen B2 (F) delivered. The final series can be identified by the ball-mounted flame projector in the hull, an extension to the fighting compartment; an additional driver-type visor and vision block for the flame projector operator; and a large armoured fuel tank over the final drive at the rear of the tank.

These Panzerkampfwagen B2 (F) were painted in dunkelgrau RAL 7021 (Dark grey). This vehicle was issued to the 7.SS Freiwilligen Gebrigs Division 'Prinz Eugen', who were fighting the partisans in Yugoslavia. The markings for 'Prinz Eugen' is painted on the forward headlight in yellow. The tactical number on the turret and the cross on the hull sides are white.

### Notes sur les planches en couleur

A1 Après l'introduction de la première série de 90 Panzerkampfwagen II (F), 150 Panzerkampfwagen II (F) supplémentaires furent commandés. En août 1941, la production de ces 2. Serie La.S.138 (2ème série) avait déjà commencé. En décembre 1941, on décida d'utiliser ces châssis pour monter le 7.62cm Pak 36(r) au lieu du Flammpanzer. Seulement 62 des Panzerkampfwagen II (F) Ausf.B avaient été terminés lorsque la production s'arrêta en mars 1942. Tous les chars terminés en 1941 furent peints en dunkelgrau RAL 7021 (gris foncé). A2 Après la décision de monter des canons antichars sur les châssis commandés pour le Panzerkampfwagen II (F) Ausf.B on dressa un nouveau plan pour continuer à produire les Flammpanzer. La première série de conversions fut obtenue en montant l'un des Flammenwerfer-SpritzKopf (tête de lance-flamme) du Panzerkampfwagen II (F) au lieu du 7.5cm sur châssis du Pz.Kmfw.B2. Les chars allemands de cette période étaient peints en dunkelgrau RAL.7021 (gris foncé) et les Panzerkampfwagen B2 (F) furent repeints dans cette couleur durant leur période de réfection.

B1 Initialement, les Sd.Kfz.251/16 furent construits sur le châssis du Sd.Kfz.251 Ausf.C. Notre sujet est basé sur le Sd.Kfz.251 Ausf.D. A cette période, le blindage allemand était peint avec une couche de base de dunkelgelb (Jaune foncé) et, si nécessaire, se vaporisait par dessus des taches et rayures irrégulières en olivgrun RAL 6003 (vert olive foncé) et de rotbraun RAL 8017 (chocolat foncé). L'intérieur était également peint en dunkelgelb (jaune foncé). B2 Deux Flammpanzer Kompanie, la 352 et la 353, étaient équipées de dix Flammpanzer 38 convertis à partir de Jagdpanzer 38 prélevés sur les lignes de production de BMM à Prague le 8 décembre 1944. Le basic rot RAL 8012 (enduit rouge) était recouvert à la main de rayures de camouflage irrégulières en olivgrun RAL 6003 (vert olive foncé) et dunkelgelb (jaune foncé) bien dilués.

C Le Panzerkampfwagen III (Fl) fut converti à partir du châssis du 100 Panzerkampfwagen III Ausf.M qui avait été fabriqué par Miag à Brausweig. On les livra à Wegmann à Kassel où ils furent terminés comme les Penzerkampfwagen III (Fl). Au total, 21 Panzerkampfwagen III (Fl) servirent en Italie. L'extérieur était peint en dunkelgelb RAL 7028 (marron) utilisé à partir de février 1943. Les Panzerkampfwagen III (Fl) de cette unité n'étaient pas camouflés.

D1 L'extérieur était peint en dunkelgelb RAL 7028 (marron) appliqué à partir de février 1943. L'équipage avait le droit d'appliquer des motifs camouflage composés de rayures et taches olivgrun RAL 6003 (vert olive foncé) et rotbraun RAL 8017 (chocolat foncé) sur le dunkelgelb de base. Les Panzerkampfwagen III (Fl) de cette unité n'étaient pas camouflés mais le numéro tactique sur la tourelle a été modifié. D2 Ce Panzerkampfwagen III (Fl), numéro tactique '851' de la 6ème Division Panzer fut muni rétrospectivement d'un Schurtzen (tablier de blindage) pour protéger les côtés de la coque des tirs antichars russes. En mai 1943, le OKH Gruppe Sud publia une liste de nouveaux symboles de division qui pouvaient être appliqués en dernière minute. On pense que les lettres 'Op' sont les initiales du commandant d'unité telles qu'elles apparaissent sur d'autres Panzerkampfwagen III Ausf.M et N de l'unité.

E Dix Sturmgeschut reconstruits furent convertis en Sturmgeschut (Flamm) en mai et juin 1943. Ce Sturmgeschut (Flamm) fut converti à partir d'un Sturmgeschut Ausf.F/8 qui était le premier Sturmgeschut à utiliser le châssis u. Serie/Z.W. introduit sur le Pz.Kpfw.III Ausf.J. Un blindage supplémentaire était soudé aux surfaces avant pour augmenter leur épaisseur à 80mm.

F Au total, 46 1.Serie Panzerkampfwagen II (F) furent construits avec le nouveau châssis La.S.138. Quelques-uns possédaient le châssis destiné au Panzerkampfwagen II Ausf.E (Fahrgestell Nr. 27801-28000). Le Ausf.E peut être identifié par sa chenille lubrifiée, qui était bien plus large que les chenilles d'acier sèches normales utilisées par les Ausf.D. Les chars livrés avant août 1940 comportaient le camouflage bicolore standard dunkelgrau RAL 7021 (gris foncé) et dunkelbrau RAL 7018 (marron foncé). A partir d'août 1940, tous les chars étaient peints seulement en dunkelgrau RAL 7021 (gris foncé).

G Il s'agit de l'une des dernières séries de production du Panzerkampfwagen B2 (F) livrées. La série finale est identifiée par le lance-flamme monté sur globe dans la coque, une extension du compartiment de combat, une visière de type pilote et un bloc vision pour l'opérateur du lance-flammes ainsi qu'un gros réservoir de carburant blindé derrière la transmission finale àl'arrière du char. Ces Panzerkampfwagen B2 (F) étaient peints en dunkelgrau RAL 7021 (gris foncé). Ce véhicule fut émis au 7.SS Freiwilligen Gebrigs Division 'Prinz Eugen' qui combattait les partisans en Yougoslavie. Le numéro tactique sur la tourelle et la croix sur les côtés de la coque sont blancs.

## Farbtafeln

A1 Nachdem die erste Serie von 90 Panzerkampfwagen II (F) produziert war, wurden weitere 150 Panzerkampfwagen II (F) bestellt. Im August 1941 war die Produktion dieser 2. Serie La.S. 138 bereits angelaufen. Im Dezember 1941 wurde beschlossen, auf diese Fahrgestelle das 7,62 cm die Pak 36 (r) anstelle des Flammpanzers zu montieren. Lediglich 62 Stück der Panzerkampfwagen II (F) Ausf. B waren fertiggestellt, als im März 1942 die Produktion eingestellt

wurde. Alle 1941 fertiggestellten Panzer wurden dunkelgrau (RAL 7021) gestrichen. A2 Nachdem man den Entschluß gefaßt hatte, auf die Fahrgestelle, die für den Panzerkampfwagen II (F) Ausf. B bestellt worden waren, Panzerabwehrgeschütze zu montieren, entstanden neue Pläne, weitere Flammpanzer herzustellen. Die erste Serien-Umrüstung bestand darin, daß man einen der Flammenwerfer-Spritzköpfe des Panzerkampfwagen II (F) anstatt des 7,5 cm vom Pz.Kpfw. B2, das auf dem Rumpf angebracht war, montierte. Die deutschen Panzer aus dieser Zeit waren dunkelgrau (RAL 7021) gestrichen, die Panzerkampfwagen B2 (F) wurden im Zuge der Umrüstung auf diese Farbe umgespritzt.

B1 Zunächst wurden die Sd.Kfz.251/16 auf das Fahrgestell der Sd.Kfz.251 Ausf.C gebaut. Unsere Abbildung beruht auf dem Sd.Kfz.251 Ausf.D. Zu dieser Zeit wurden deutsche Panzerwagen mit einer dunkelgelben Grundschicht versehen. Falls erforderlich, wurde diese mit unregelmäßigen Farbflecken und Streifen in olivgrün (RAL 6003) und rotbraun (RAL 8017) überspritzt. Auch das Innere war dunkelgelb gestrichen. B2 Zwei Flammpanzer-Kompanien, die 352. und die 353., waren jeweils mit 10 Flammpanzern 38 ausgerüstet, bei denen es sich um umgerüstete Jagdpanzer 38 handelte, die am 8. Dezember 1944 aus der Produktion der BMM in Prag liefen. Der rote Grundierlack (RAL 8012) wurde von Hand mit unregelmäßigen Tarnstreifen in stark verdünnter, olivgrüner (RAL 6003) und dunkelgelber Farbe überstrichen.

C Der Panzerkampfwagen III (Fl) wurde aus 100 Fahrgestellen des Panzerkampfwagen III Ausf.M umgerüstet, die von Miag in Braunschweig gefertigt worden waren. Sie wurden an Wegmann in Kassel geliefert, wo sie als Panzerkampfwagen III (Fl) fertiggestellt wurden. Insgesamt wurden 21 Panzerkampfwagen III (Fl) in Italien eingesetzt. Außen waren sie dunkelgelb (RAL 7028) gespritzt, wie ab Februar 1943 gebräuchlich. Die Panzerkampfwagen III (Fl) dieser Einheit hatten kein Tarnmuster.

D1 Das Äußere war dunkelgelb (RAL 7028), wie ab Februar 1943 gebräuchlich, gespritzt. Es war den Mannschaften gestattet, Tarnmuster mit Streifen und Farbflecken in olivgrün (RAL 6003) und rotbraun (RAL 8017) über die dunkelgelbe Grundfarbe aufzutragen. Die Panzerkampfwagen III (Fl) dieser Einheit hatten kein Tarnmuster, doch die taktische Nummer auf dem Gefechtssturm wurde abgeändert. D2 Dieser Panzerkampfwagen III (Fl), taktische Nummer "851", der 6. Panzerdivision wurde nachträglich mit sogenannten Schürzen ausgestattet, die den Rumpf seitlich vor dem Beschuß der Russen mit Panzerjägergeschützen schützen sollten. Im Mai 1943 gab die OKH Gruppe Süd eine Liste mit neuen Divisionsabzeichen heraus, die kurzfristig aufgetragen werden konnten. Bei den Buchstaben "Op" handelt es sich wahrscheinlich um die Initialen des Befehlshabers der Einheit, da sie auch auf anderen Panzerkampfwagen III Ausf.M und N dieser Einheit auftauchen.

E Zehn umgebaute Sturmgeschütze wurden im Mai und Juni 1943 zu Sturmgeschütz (Flamm) umgerüstet. Dieses Sturmgeschütz (Flamm) entstand aus einem Sturmgeschütz Ausf.F/8, das erste Sturmgeschütz, bei dem das Fahrgestell der 8. Serie/Z.W. zum Einsatz kam, das beim Pz.Kpfw.III Ausf.J eingeführt worden war. An den vorderen Flächen wurde eine zusätzliche Panzerung angeschweißt, wodurch sie eine Dicke von 80 mm erreichten.

F Insgesamt wurden 46 1.Serie-Panzerkampfwagen II (F) mit dem neuen Fahrgestell La.S. 138 gebaut. Bei einigen davon handelte es sich um die Fahrgestelle, die für den Panzerkampfwagen II Ausf.E (Fahrgestell-Nr. 27801-28000) entwickelt worden waren. Die Ausf.E zeichnet sich durch die geschmierte Kette aus, die viel tiefer war als die normale Trockenstiftstahlkette, die bei der Ausf.D benutzt wurde. Panzer, die vor August 1940 ausgeliefert wurden, hatten das standardmäßige, zweifarbige Tarnmuster in dunkelgrau (RAL 7021) und dunkelbraun (RAL 7018). Ab August 1940 wurden alle Panzer nur noch dunkelgrau (RAL 7021) gespritzt.

G Dies ist eine der letzten Produktionsserien von Panzerkampfwagen B2 (F), die ausgeliefert wurden. Die letzte Serie unterscheidet sich von den anderen durch den Kugellager-Flammenwerfer im Rumpf, eine Erweiterung des Gefechtsabteils, einen zusätzlichen Blendschirm im Fahrerstil und einen Sichtblock für den Bediener des Flammenwerfers; außerdem hatte diese Serie einen großen, gepanzerten Brennstofftank über dem letzten Kettenlager auf der Rückseite des Panzers. Diese Panzerkampfwagen B2 (F) waren dunkelgrau (RAL 7021) gestrichen. Dieses Fahrzeug wurde der 7. SS Freiwilligen Gebirgsdivision "Prinz Eugen" überstellt, die gegen die Partisanen in Jugoslawien kämpften. Die taktische Nummer auf dem Gefechtssturm und das Kreuz auf den beiden Rumpfseiten sind weiß.